KU-751-736

A TIME TO RECEIVE

A Time to Receive

A Prayer Course for
Everyday Use

Lavinia Byrne IBVM

Hodder & Stoughton
LONDON SYDNEY AUCKLAND

[Scripture quotations are] from the New Revised Standard Version
Bible, Anglicised Edition, copyright ©1989, 1995. Division of
Christian Education of the National Council of the Churches of
Christ in the USA. All rights reserved.

The extracts from R. S. Thomas's *The Bush* and W. H. Auden's
Stop All the Clocks have been used by kind permission of
Faber and Faber Ltd.

Copyright © 1997 by Lavinia Byrne

The right of Lavinia Byrne to be identified as the Author of
the Work has been asserted by her in accordance with the
Copyright, Designs and Patents Act 1988.

First published in Great Britain in 1997
Second edition published November 1997

10 9 8 7 6 5 4 3 2 1

All rights reserved. No part of this publication may be
reproduced, stored in a retrieval system, or transmitted,
in any form or by any means without the prior written
permission of the publisher, nor be otherwise circulated
in any form of binding or cover other than that in which
it is published and without a similar condition being
imposed on the subsequent purchaser.

British Library Cataloguing in Publication Data
A record for this book is available from the British Library

ISBN 0 340 69474 2

Typeset by Avon Dataset Ltd, Bidford-on-Avon, Warks.

Printed and bound in Great Britain by
Mackays of Chatham PLC, Chatham, Kent

Hodder and Stoughton
A division of Hodder Headline PLC
338 Euston Road
London NW1 3BH

Introduction

This is a book about prayer which will help you pray. It began life as a BBC Lent course but has now been adapted for everyday use. You can start it when you want, but ideally on a Sunday so that it can run for six whole weeks. It follows the form of the Lord's Prayer which begins with the word 'Father'.

The Lord's Prayer

The Lord's Prayer is the central Christian prayer, the unique prayer of encounter with God. It puts God first; it focuses on our relationship with God. It engages with what concerns us most deeply. It invites us to follow Jesus in spirit, truth and service. It reminds us that we need food and forgiveness. It holds up to us a mirror into which we can look at times of depression and despair. 'Father', it says, and then names God's attributes of holiness and glory. It identifies our deepest hopes and desires by having us pray for the coming of the kingdom and for our daily bread. It names our fears – of sin, of our own fragility, of temptation and trial. It is not simply for the glory moments of our life. It is Jesus's prayer and now it can become ours too.

But this requires a certain freedom of the heart. Can we throw off some of the old associations of school prayers, chanting voices that get the words out but never really let them in? Can we engage with the text in a new way?

Maybe we can by using an unfamiliar version of the Lord's Prayer. It is from Luke's Gospel and this is how it goes:

Father,
hallowed be your name.
Your kingdom come.
Give us each day our daily bread.
And forgive us our sins,
for we ourselves forgive
everyone indebted to us.
And do not bring us to the time of trial.

Luke 11:2–4

So what is 'missing'? The 'Our' for starters, and then the 'who art in heaven' and the 'thy will be done on earth as it is in heaven'. The second half of the prayer is different too. It does not make forgiveness conditional on our ability to forgive those who 'trespass against us'. It is streamlined, simple, austere even.

The version of the Lord's Prayer we know by heart is taken from Matthew 6:9–13; this one is from Luke. And that makes a difference because the picture each gospel writer gives of Jesus is unique. Matthew's Jesus is the great teacher of the Sermon on the Mount. Mark's Jesus rushes about unsettling people. John's is lofty, the eternal word made flesh. And Luke's? Luke's Jesus is the friend of ordinary people. He bears our burdens and lightens the load on our spirits. He is concerned with the many and not simply the few. He brings the gospel to the Gentiles, to women and children, the sick, the lonely and the poor. He has Mary sing the Magnificat and Zechariah the Benedictus. In chapter 11 he teaches his followers how to pray.

We are told that he was praying in a certain place and that they said to him, 'Teach us how to pray.' 'When you pray,' Jesus replies, 'say "Father" . . .' That sounds effortless, doesn't it? When you pray, do it simply and directly. Simply do it, like riding a bicycle or falling off a log. You do not have to go out and buy the starter pack. You do not have to have a special set of clothes, or the software, or the trainers. All you do is say 'Father'. Open your mind and heart to God. And go with the flow of what happens next.

Naming God

When you know the right name for someone, you can enjoy a unique relationship with them. The earliest account of creation in the Bible gives an extraordinary task to Adam. He has to name the birds and the animals. The book of Genesis takes up the story. 'So out of the ground the Lord God formed every animal of the field and every bird of the air, and brought them to the man to see what he would call them; and whatever the man called every living creature, that was its name' (Genesis 2:19). There is huge authority and power here and also a sense of loss, for when the man names the birds and animals, and gives them each a distinct identity, he then realises that he has no mate among them. They are distinctive and different from him, but true companionship will only come with a fellow human being, God's further gift to him of Eve.

The truly wise know how to name accurately. That is why the business of naming God is taken so seriously in every religion. When you get God's name or names sorted, you enter into a relationship with the Divine. You stand on holy ground.

The greatest teachers of prayer have taken this bit of their task extraordinarily seriously. So within the Christian tradition, for instance, no prayer is held in more esteem than the Lord's Prayer, the prayer Jesus taught his followers. It begins by naming God.

That first naming releases so many other associations. Once you have found the name God has for you, you stand on holy but also on firm ground. Now is that a slip of the tongue, or what? 'Once you have found the name God has for you' can be heard two different ways round. God has a distinctive name, but so too do we. If you call God 'Father', then you are also naming yourself as the beloved daughter or son of God. If you call God by a name that conveys mystery, you are attempting to grasp something of the mystery of your own being. If you call God by a name which identifies a virtue, 'mercy' or 'compassion', for example, then you are setting yourself a task for your very being will also be called to echo the qualities you name in God and to show them forth in your own life. Naming

God is one of the most serious things we ever do. When we name God, we identify ourselves. We open ourselves to receive our identity from the one whom we name.

Holiness

When I was a child I was absolutely convinced I knew what holiness was. It meant being good, never complaining, drinking the milk in my cereal and not pouring it back into the jug on the sly, washing when I was told to – especially my teeth – saying my prayers, picking up my clothes, and not making gunpowder in the cellar like my brother who had a nasty accident and was taken to hospital. I'll never forget the flash of fire and the sound of the explosion he made. He ran up the cellar steps crying out in pain. And only the day before I'd been with him watching in fascination as the yellow and black powders swirled round in his mortar and pestle, oblivious to the real danger of mixing saltpetre, sulphur and charcoal.

Would that life had remained so cut and dried. Would that my world had remained so safe and comforting, with 'being good' as the ultimate guide and goal, and nice measurable things like tidy clothes and clean teeth to assess my achievements by. Nowadays I realise that being holy is both a much more complicated and a much more simple affair. Complicated because, at times, my life feels a total mess, and this depresses me. I have failed totally to keep my life as orderly as my clothes, or as clean as my teeth. That is the problem with a view of holiness which sees it as something we do for ourselves, rather than as something which God does for us.

Holiness is simple too because of its true nature. In the Lord's Prayer we repeat the words Jesus taught his followers to use as they prayed: 'hallowed be your name.' It is the name of God which is holy; God is holy. Any holiness we have is mediated to us. In essence we are moons, rather than suns. We do not shine on our own account. All our holiness is derived from the holiness of God.

This gives a huge simplicity to human living. All is grace; all is gift. And God is the giver. We are to co-operate, just as the moon co-operates by swinging through its appointed orbit and picking up and mirroring back the sun's great light to the earth.

So what is the sun's great light? The moon would be invisible without it. It would not appear; it would seem to have no existence. Whereas in the light of the sun, the moon seems radiant. This is what union with God looks like. It is about closeness and growth and fruitfulness. It is about core identity, about our very being, and our development as the beloved of God. It is about total freedom and total dependency, about grace and life and energy and love.

That is why our lives give glory to God when we spin in our true orbit. Our humanity is swept into relationship with God and we display the source of our deepest identity with our every word and gesture and deed. We mirror the divine image and likeness. And, because of the transformation which is realised in us, other people can look at us and know what God is like.

That is the simple bit, simple because if we really believed it, our lives would be deeply simplified. Whereas, because of the complexity of human frailty and sin, we struggle with the adult equivalent of pouring the milk out of cereal back into the jug and making gunpowder in the cellar. Life becomes a complicated mess as we pour things back into containers where they no longer fit, or mix them in toxic solutions in our own underworlds.

Every time I pray 'Hallowed by thy name' I hope I am praying to be released from the tyranny of my own perfectionism and restored to true light of my identity before God. Then I can spin like the moon and forget the lure of an artificial, explosive, self-igniting light.

Your Kingdom Come

A journalist laughed at me. She came to interview me and laughed at the way I'd got books lined up in my bedroom. They are sorted by colour, you see. After all, one of the most memorable things about a book is the colour of its jacket. So my logic is quite sound. If I know my Bible has a blue spine, I'll search for it amongst the blue books. And my dictionary of

computers and my dictionary of quotations stand either side of
it, one a slightly darker, one a slightly paler shade of blue. I
guess that's the problem about letting someone into your
bedroom. Once they come in, they see all your little private
quirks and fancies – and then you run the risk that they will
laugh at you, even in a good-humoured way.

If you live constantly in public, you can, as it were, control
your image and the way in which you are publicly perceived. In
your own room, however, you become a private person, whatever
the roles and responsibilities you fulfil in the public domain.

Is that why Jesus has such firm instructions about prayer?
'Whenever you pray, go into your room and shut the door and
pray to your Father who is in secret; and your Father who sees
in secret will reward you (Matthew 6:6). Jesus calls us to prayer.
In this account, from Matthew's Gospel, we discover that prayer
is a deeply personal experience, one which requires us to go
into our room and shut the door. What does this mean?

Inside your own room you find the time and space and
opportunity to become reflective. That is why we are commanded
to pray to God who is in secret. Our own room becomes the
place where our deep desires are met by God. So what are your
deepest desires?

Desires are tricky because most of us have been taught to be
afraid of them. But suppose that God speaks to us in what we
most seek? In the Lord's Prayer, for instance, we pray, 'Your
kingdom come.' Now that's a prayer that matches our deepest
desires. We want the world to be a place of justice and peace
and truth. And we should be fearless about identifying that
desire.

The meeting with God is the reward of prayer. It makes you
more yourself because you become closer to God's love of you.
That is why Jesus wanted us to pray in secret and to take the
risk of encountering our deepest desires. The hypocritical prayer is the person who does not take the risk of true encounter
whereas the person who prays alone will meet God. Before you
begin this prayer course, take the time to identify your own
deep desires. Try to identify three graces which you want to

pray for. Make them be really important. Spend time over them and then write them down on a piece of paper, one which you can put somewhere safe or somewhere where you will be able to find it again. Think about them each day, keep them by you, on your desk, in your kitchen or on your dashboard, and remember to pray for them.

Our Daily Bread

My community in North London is fairly international. There are sisters in the group who have worked in Africa, Canada, the States and Australia. We have an occasional Korean evening, with food prepared by a sister from Seoul. Last year, Prisca, who came from Kerala in South India, would prepare curries for us. Food is such an important marker. It's a kind of shorthand which tells you a huge amount about people, about the way they live, what they cultivate, their climate, their attitudes even. There's a lot of truth in the old adage that we are what we eat.

So I'm struck by our Muslim cook, Aisha. She keeps Ramadan. And yet she solemnly cooks for the sisters all through this time. Now Aisha is a Scot, brought up in Glasgow. One day in Ramadan she told me about her grandmother who kept bees. I felt guilty for making her think about the delights of eating honey at such a sacred time. I shouldn't have worried. I should have thought about the true meaning of fasting. After all, Jesus has me pray, 'Give us today our daily bread,' which means thinking carefully about food and my attitudes towards it.

We do not grow towards God in isolation from other people, but always with them. Eating is a shared activity. And so is fasting too. What do we really think about hunger and about food and about human need of companionship? What most nourishes us? You cannot pray for God's kingdom to come, you cannot ask for daily bread and you cannot ask for forgiveness independently of each other. All three belong together and are the response in faith of a truly loving heart. That is where the wisdom of the Lord's Prayer lies.

And Forgive Us Our Sins, For We Ourselves Forgive Everyone Indebted to Us

It has further wisdom too because it speaks to our own condition. We want to be forgiven and we want to forgive. We know that hatred and rancour devour our energy, that family or national or world conflict sap the sources of our well-being. Yet the dilemma of seeking true forgiveness and for a just solution to our problems is one which subtly evades us. Do we really believe that God wants our good? Do we really believe that the world can be rebuilt in ways that respect the needs of the human family? What are our attitudes to debt and to forgiveness? Can Jesus help us look at these questions with something approaching sanity or are we almost bound to get wrapped up in guilt as we try to think about them?

Conflict is terrible. Any lack of freedom is a travesty of our identity as the beloved of God. We live in a culture that puts the young in debt, mortgages the life of the middle-aged and terrifies the elderly with penury. How can we regain freedom?

The Time of Trial

The desire to pray is deeply, deeply rooted in us, whatever our faith tradition. The most important question any disciple can ask of a spiritual teacher is 'How can I pray?'; the greatest act of personal trust is to say to someone whom you believe to be close to God 'Teach me to pray.' That must be why the followers of Jesus asked him how they were to pray. They trusted that he would give them a good answer – one which would be authentic but also one which would be realistic.

For this reason we are told to pray that we may not be brought to the time of trial. True testing and true trial are like the fire that purifies by searing us to the soul. We are destroyed and remade in the same blast. And the destruction can be devastating. That is why any serious experience of the Lord's Prayer brings us into a new relationship with the life, suffering and death of Jesus. The pattern of his passion will be replicated in ours. It will bring us to the foot of the cross and to the joy of his resurrection.

A Time to Receive

Every meeting with God takes place within time. It is not a disembodied experience which happens in some kind of spiritual mailbox, out of sight and out of mind, for us to call by and check out when we are in the mood. Time is critical to human living. Without it we would not be. That is why we do things to mark its beginnings and its ends: academic and financial years, births and deaths, and of course birthdays and anniversaries. We put down mental markers and surround them with cards and presents and cakes and candles, ritualising the passage of time. The human year is governed by the movement of the sun and the moon which mete out light to us and guide our tides, giving us seasons for sowing and seasons for reaping. Then there are the imaginary markers which vary for all of us but which are addressed by the Chinese proverb which says, 'If you think in seasons, plant cereal crops; if you think in decades, plant trees; if you think in centuries, educate your children.' That requires no commentary. It speaks quite simply and directly to our perspective on eternity.

We do want to live, we do want to endure. And we know that timing is all. That is why the meeting with God takes place within time and why our use of time for our own spiritual development is not an arbitrary affair. Ritual and liturgy are as old as religion itself. When human beings start looking for God, they set time aside for the quest. When they find God, they put markers up. They organise a liturgical year, a cycle of prayer, a daily routine.

This is what this book offers with reflections on the words of prayer which Jesus taught his followers. It was more than a prayer to him; it was the pattern of his whole identity. And so too can it become of ours.

Martha and Mary

But surely, you might object, there are different styles of prayer. And how are we to know if we are getting in right? At the end of chapter 10 of Luke's Gospel, just before the passage we are praying with, there is a story which gives the context for Jesus's teaching on prayer, and which can set our minds at rest. The story is of his visit to the house of two sisters, Martha and Mary. Martha runs around in the kitchen, while Mary sits at the feet of Jesus and listens to him. Scripture commentators have been hard on Martha. After all, Jesus himself seems to give Mary all the accolades. She 'has chosen the better part'. Traditionally this has been used as a proof text to demonstrate that people who pray – people who sit in wordless adoration contemplating Jesus – are better than the rest of us, the doers who have no choice, if truth be told, but to beaver away in the kitchen or wherever we do our own personal hard graft. Prayer and work get separated by this reading of the text. Mary wins; Martha comes a rather poor second.

But read the text again (in Luke 10:38–42). This is a story about all of us. We all have a Martha and a Mary inside ourselves. It is Martha who invites Jesus in. Martha makes the contemplation possible. And she is generous, opening her home to Jesus. This is her reality. Her dozy sister, meanwhile, has a different role in the story. She sits at the Rabbi's feet in the position of discipleship. She is going to learn from him. How? By *listening*. Martha forgets to listen and starts getting hot and bothered. That is when she flies off the handle and starts rampaging around inside her kitchen and then flares up and shouts at Jesus. There is tension and division within this story. But the division is not between pray-ers and workers. It is between people who remember to listen to Jesus and those who forget. And you can listen anywhere. That is the whole point.

So how are you going to listen to God? How are you, like Martha, going to invite Jesus into your home? Into your human reality as it is. Be realistic. Set time aside but don't set yourself an impossible target which is not doable. Notice what helps, what doesn't help. Read the material set for prayer each day. Use it as a springboard. Then let Mary take over – the attentive disciple who wants to work with Martha and not against her, and who knows that you have to listen, whether you are driving, cooking, ironing, cleaning, in the bath, going to work, going to school, eating, sitting at a computer screen or absent-mindedly doing most or all of these things at once. Listening is all. Then, as Jesus says to all his followers, both then and now, start by saying 'Father,' . . . and your prayer has begun.

Use the exercises in this book as they help you. Use the reflections because they will feed your prayer. And, above all, use the passages of Scripture which are set for daily reading. If you want to share some of what you discover with a group of friends, the book can also be followed by a community of people as well. Feel free to adapt it, to modify the pace, to repeat and go back to your favourite hymns and prayers, to go over your best exercises or to do the ones which bothered you again. Use the material over and over again and let it help you so that your own personal prayer course becomes a time for you to receive great graces from God.

This book was prepared with help and encouragement from many people in the BBC's Religious Programmes Department. I thank the Head of Department, Ernest Rea, as a way of thanking them all. Angela Tilby read the original manuscript with a critical and wise eye. Keith Riglin helped with information about hymns and a disk of collects. I thank Christopher and Tina Lamb in Wales and the IBVM community in Hampstead for their hospitality while I was writing, and Judith Longman from Hodder & Stoughton for her customary editorial expertise.

Lavinia Byrne IBVM

1st Sunday – The Revelation of God as Father

Jesus's prayer begins 'Father.' What resonances does that word carry in the Christian imagination? Here is a parable where the word 'father' occurs thirteen times. What does it tell us about God?

Scripture Reading

Then Jesus said, 'There was a man who had two sons. The younger of them said to his father, "Father, give me the share of the property that will belong to me." So he divided his property between them. A few days later the younger son gathered all he had and travelled to a distant country, and there he squandered his property in dissolute living. When he had spent everything, a severe famine took place throughout that country, and he began to be in need. So he went and hired himself out to one of the citizens of that country, who sent him to his fields to feed the pigs. He would gladly have filled himself with the pods that the pigs were eating; and no one gave him anything. But when he came to himself he said, "How many of my father's hired hands have bread enough and to spare, but here I am dying of hunger! I will get up and go to my father, and I will say to him, 'Father, I have sinned against heaven and before you; I am no longer worthy to be called your son; treat me like one of your hired hands.' " So he set off and went to his father. But while he was still far off, his father saw him and was filled with compassion; he ran and put his arms around him and kissed him. Then the son said to him, "Father, I have sinned against heaven and before you; I am no longer worthy to be called your son." But the father said to his slaves, "Quickly, bring out a robe – the best one – and put it on him; put a ring on his finger and sandals on his feet. And get the fatted calf and kill it, and let us eat and celebrate; for this son of mine was dead and is alive again; he was lost and is found!" And they began to celebrate.

'Now his elder son was in the field; and when he came and approached the house, he heard music and dancing. He called one of the slaves and asked what was going on. He replied, "Your brother has come, and your father has killed the fatted calf, because he has got him back safe and sound." He became angry and refused to go in. His father came out and began to plead with him. He answered his father, "Listen! For all these years I have been working like a slave for you, and I have never disobeyed your command; yet you have never given me even a young goat so that I might celebrate with my friends. But when this son of yours came back, who has devoured your property with prostitutes, you killed the fatted calf for him!" Then the father said to him, "Son, you are always with me, and all that is mine is yours. But we had to celebrate and rejoice, because this brother of yours was dead and has come to life; he was lost and has been found." ' (Luke 15:11–32)

Reflection

There are three parables about being lost and found in Luke 15: the lost sheep, the lost coin and the lost son. Luke tells them with extraordinary narrative verve. He has a film-maker's flair for focusing now on one character, now on another. We listen to the younger son as he demands his inheritance and then follow him into exile as he heads for a distant country. We join him in the fields as hunger brings him to his senses. But then the camera cuts to the father and the whole mood of the story changes.

For the father is driven totally by love, whereas the son had looked to his rights and privileges. He had traded on his rights as a son by demanding access to his inheritance or property. He had traded his very being by selling himself into slavery. His elder brother, as we subsequently discover, is also in a total mess. He too has worked 'like a slave'. He cannot bring himself to call his father by name and refers to his brother as 'this son of yours'. He may have stayed at home whilst his brother wandered off, but his saga is identical. What both brothers have lost is their sense of being loved unconditionally, with the kind of love which is unique to parents. 'Am I a slave? Am I a son?' they worry. The younger brother keeps insisting on what he will tell his father: 'I will get up and go to my father and say . . .' The elder brother is even more blunt: 'Listen,' he says and then pours out his fury and rage.

Salvation lies in hearing what the father wants. For he is the God of abundance who gives us an identity which does not have to be negotiated. All is gift. We are held in the embrace of God. Listen to God now. Listen to the word of Jesus and rejoice. Join the father in the gospel parable as he runs down the road towards you: 'But while he was still far off, his father saw him and was filled with compassion; he ran and put his arms around him and kissed him.'

When we pray the version of the Lord's Prayer which begins 'Father', we ourselves run towards this embrace.

Prayer

O Parent of parents and Friend of all friends, without entreaty you took into your care, and by degrees led me from all else that at length I might see and settle my love in you. O happily begun freedom. The beginning of all my good, and more worth to me than the whole world besides.

Mary Ward, 1585–1645

Exercise

Say Luke's version of the Lord's Prayer very slowly. Experience its simplicity. Now repeat it pretending that you are the elder son in the parable. Then repeat it again, only this time let yourself be the younger son. Listen to God. (The prayer is written out in full on page 4.)

Monday – Week One:
Jesus Calls God 'Father'

We learn who God is from Jesus.

Scripture Reading

At that same hour Jesus rejoiced in the Holy Spirit and said, 'I thank you, Father, Lord of heaven and earth, because you have hidden these things from the wise and the intelligent and have revealed them to infants; yes, Father, for such was your gracious will. All things have been handed over to me by my Father; and no one knows who the Son is except the Father, or who the Father is except the Son and anyone to whom the Son chooses to reveal him.' (Luke 10:21–22)

Reflection

This is Jesus's third reference to the Father in Luke's gospel. He gradually builds up a picture for us, an identikit portrait of God. The first comes in Luke 6:36: 'Be merciful, just as your Father is merciful.' God is introduced as the source of all mercy, the loving Father of yesterday's parable. Matthew has a matching verse to this one, a text whose focus is sufficiently different to demonstrate just how distinctive Luke's gospel is. For in Matthew, at the end of the Sermon on the Mount, we read: 'Be perfect, therefore, as your heavenly Father is perfect' (Matthew 5:48). For Matthew's perfection – with its overtones of the Law – we have Luke's clemency and mercy. God the Father of Jesus is a God of forgiveness, a God who wants us to become forgiving, loving people.

The second reference is provided by Luke 9:26: 'Those who are ashamed of me and of my words, of them the Son of Man will be ashamed when he comes in his glory and the glory of the Father and of the holy angels.' This text uses the language of revelation and of glory. Intimacy gives way to glory. If there is a sense of judgement, the gospel here suggests that it will be based not on one's good works, but upon fidelity to Jesus and to his word. At the final revelation, when Jesus comes in glory, the only test which will be applied is the test of faith. We will be asked if we believed in him, and if the answer is 'yes', then we will share his glory. And if we have to say that we were ashamed to believe in him, that the message was a bit too simple for us, because it was such an uncomplicated one about the love of God and the mercy of God, then Jesus, the Son of Man, will be ashamed of us and we will not share his glory.

Today's reading reminds us that knowing about God's desire to be intimate and merciful with us is not restricted to an elite. This is not specialised learning, a way of life for the wise and the intelligent. If anything such knowledge is more accessible to infants than to complicated people. In Luke's version, Jesus brings the good news of God's love to learners, to people who are like us and not to people who are unlike us. Sinners, the desolate, those who are weighed down by their experience, and especially by the judgement of others all find a welcome here. It is not by chance that the first characters who come to the crib are shepherds in this gospel and that Jesus dies between two criminals.

When Jesus reveals God to us, we learn that the Father is full of mercy and full of glory. But, above all, we learn that God desires to be known. Intimacy and glory are wrapped up in each other. And within God, we will find both. Our task is to believe that.

Prayer

O Father, give the spirit power to climb
To the fountain of all light, and be purified.
Break through the mists of earth, the weight of the clod,

Shine forth in splendour, thou that art calm weather,
And quiet resting place for faithful souls.
To see thee is the end and the beginning,
Thou carriest us, and thou dost go before.
Thou art the journey, and the journey's end.
        Boethius, 480–524, tr. Helen Waddell, 1889–1965

Father, you have made us for yourself and our hearts are restless
until they rest in you. In all our trials and crises, recall us to the
true nature and purpose of our lives, that again and again we
may come to the end of ourselves and find you there still holding
and sustaining us in the depths. Amen.

God, who made us to worship you
    in the tangle of our minds,
We praise and bless you for those
    whose clarity of thought
      leaves us in light and hope.
We know such clarity is often hard-won,
    and hewn painfully,
      piece by piece
from the rocks of doubt and uncertainty.
Give our thinkers, we pray,
    the boldness to question
    and to dream,
that your beauty and peace
    may dawn in our minds
through Jesus Christ, our Lord, Amen.
        Christopher A. Lamb, 1939–

Exercise

Find Luke's next reference to the word 'Father' in his gospel. If
you want a hint, try Luke 11:2. Are you surprised!

Tuesday – Week One: God of Relationships

The word 'Father' as a name for God is unique to Christianity. What does it tell us about life within the Godhead?

Scripture Reading

For all who are led by the Spirit of God are children of God. For you did not receive a spirit of slavery to fall back into fear, but you have received a spirit of adoption. When we cry, 'Abba! Father!' it is that very Spirit bearing witness with our spirit that we are children of God, and if children, then heirs, heirs of God and joint heirs with Christ – if, in fact, we suffer with him so that we may also be glorified with him. (Romans 8:14–17)

Reflection

The Spirit teaches us what it is to be the child of God. Paul, in his Letter to the Romans, is concerned to demonstrate that there are two ways of being a follower of Jesus. One is the spirit of fear or slavery. This leads us to work too hard at being good, to try to earn God's attention and so constantly to feel judged. The other is the spirit of adoption which allows us, indeed makes us, call on God with the words 'Abba, Father!'

These words are unique to Christianity. It is because Jesus called God 'Father' that we may call God 'Father'. The Creed teaches us that Jesus is the second person of the Blessed Trinity, the only-begotten Son who is sent by the Father and who, in turn, sends the Holy Spirit into the world for our salvation. These are not dry words. They explain the theological truth which inspires all human relationships and all the relationships we have with God.

Jesus can call God 'Father', we can all call God 'Father' because, at the heart of Christianity, there lies the threefold God revealed to us as Trinity. A God who is constantly in movement, constantly bent in love towards human need, towards the creation, redemption and sanctification of all that is made. Light from light. Very God of very God. The word 'Father' for God is sometimes used to show God's intimacy with us, the immanence of a God who comes into our world. But it is just as important to see it as an image of the sheer otherness and transcendence of God. God is set apart from us because the primary relationship is that which exists from eternity within the Godhead. That is where the relationships between the creator, the Redeemer and the Sanctifier were first established and lived. Then, within time, they were revealed in the life, death and resurrection of Jesus.

That is why Paul says, 'If we suffer with him, we will rise with him.' The theological mysteries of the life of Jesus are not like a movie screen which we watch and which tells us a story. They are events which become part of us. We live them too. We are born, we go down into the waters of baptism with Jesus, we suffer, die and rise again with him.

Prayers

> I bind unto myself today
> the strong name of the Trinity,
> by invocation of the same,
> the Three in One and One in Three.
>
> I bind unto myself today
> the virtues of the starlit heaven,
> the glorious sun's life-giving ray,
> the whiteness of the moon at even,
> the flashing of the lightning free,
> the whirling wind's tempestuous shocks,

the stable earth, the deep salt sea
around the old eternal rocks.

I bind unto myself the name,
the strong name of the Trinity;
by invocation of the same;
the Three in One, the One in Three,
of whom all nature has creation,
eternal Father, Spirit, Word.
Praise to the Lord of my salvation:
salvation is of Christ the Lord.
                   Patrick, 386–460, tr. Cecil Frances Alexander, 1818–95

Almighty and everlasting God,
you have given us your servants grace,
by the confession of a true faith
to acknowledge the glory of the eternal Trinity,
and in the power of the Divine Majesty to worship the Unity.
Keep us steadfast in this faith,
that we may evermore be defended from all adversities;
through Jesus Christ our Lord,
who is alive and reigns with you and the Holy Spirit,
one God, now and for ever, Amen.
                                        Collect for Trinity Sunday, ASB

Exercise

Read slowly the sixth-century hymn, known as the 'Breastplate of St Patrick'. Which lines speak to you most vividly of the nearness and the otherness of God? Then write down your favourite words of it and use them to reflect on God's care and protection of you.

Wednesday – Week One: The Passion and Desire of God

What does revelation mean? What does it mean to say that God wants to be known? The fire of God's passion made the bush burn and called Moses to new life on holy ground.

Scripture Reading

Moses was keeping the flock of his father-in-law Jethro, the priest of Midian; he led his flock beyond the wilderness, and came to Horeb, the mountain of God. There the angel of the Lord appeared to him in a flame of fire out of a bush; he looked, and the bush was blazing, yet it was not consumed. Then Moses said, 'I must turn aside and look at this great sight, and see why the bush is not burned up.' When the Lord saw that he had turned aside to see, God called to him out of the bush, 'Moses, Moses!' And he said, 'Here I am.' Then he said, 'Come no closer! Remove the sandals from your feet, for the place on which you are standing is holy ground.' He said further, 'I am the God of your father, the God of Abraham, the God of Isaac, and the God of Jacob.' And Moses hid his face, for he was afraid to look at God. (Exodus 3:1–6)

Reflection

Moses was keeping the flock. Like David who was guarding his father's sheep when Samuel came to anoint him as king, Moses is called to the encounter with God while in the midst of his everyday tasks. His father-in-law Jethro is a pagan priest, Moses the Israelite has murdered a man. He is not the most pure or perfect of individuals. Yet he is the man on whom God's eye lights. And the encounter takes place on Horeb, also known as Mount Sinai, the place where God will later reveal the Law. That is why Horeb is called the mountain of God. It is a place of disclosure, of revelation; a place where God wants to be known by name.

So what does God do? He leaps at Moses out of the burning bush. He seizes fire and waves it at Moses. He takes a risk. After all, Moses might not see, or might not be curious, or might be tired, or might be worried about the sheep. Either way, God takes the initiative and calls Moses to an encounter. And Moses does see. He turns aside at this great sight. And then he hears the voice of God, calling him by name. 'Here I am,' says Moses, as he walks towards the flaming bush. And at that moment God says, 'Come no closer.' The blaze of God's glory could harm Moses, so he must not be exposed to its radiance. But he can hear the name of God, so God speaks again: 'I am the God of your father, the God of Abraham, the God of Isaac, and the God of Jacob.'

The familiar and the unfamiliar meet. Abraham, Isaac and Jacob are part of Moses' past. He knows about them. He can tell their story. But what of this God who towers over them all? At this, Moses hides his face.

When Jesus tells us to call God 'Father', that is the experience he would have us recall. The meeting of the familiar and the unfamiliar. Of the intimate and the transcendent. Of the well-known bush and the glorious glow of God's holy fire. Of the sense of story and continuity with our own past, but equally of the overwhelming meaning and purpose behind the everyday sequence of events. There is nothing banal or trivial here, but all is transformed. Not only do the events and the patterns of our lives come together, but we learn that God desires to be known. God feels passionate about us and calls us to a burning bush. In R. S. Thomas's words, 'I know that bush/ Moses: there are many of them/ in Wales in the autumn, braziers/ where the imagination/ warms itself.' And so the very place of meeting becomes a holy place. God has spoken to Moses, to us; nothing will ever be the same again. Our imaginations flame.

Prayer

> Holy, holy, holy,
> God of power and might;
> Heaven and earth are full of your glory.
> Hosanna in the highest.
> Blessed is he who comes in the name of the Lord.
> Hosanna in the highest.
>
> Shared text of the Sanctus

> O gladsome light, O grace
> Of God the Father's face,
> The eternal splendour wearing;
> Celestial, holy, blest,
> Our Saviour Jesus Christ,
> Joyful in thine appearing.
>
> Now ere day fadeth quite,
> We see the evening light,
> Our wonted hymn outpouring;
> Father of might unknown,
> Thee, his incarnate Son,
> And Holy Spirit adoring.
>
> To thee of right belongs
> All praise of holy songs,
> O Son of God, lifegiver;
> Thee, therefore, O Most High,
> The world doth glorify,
> And shall exalt for ever.
>
> Evening Prayer, ASB

Exercise

Light a candle. Feel its heat. Say the words 'Holy, holy, holy'. Blow it out.

Thursday – Week One: Other Names for God

Once we know what the word 'Father' means and how it brings us to an encounter with the holiness and otherness of God, then it becomes safe to experiment with other names for God.

Scripture Reading

Blessed be the Lord, my rock, who trains my hands for war, and my fingers for battle; my rock and my fortress, my stronghold and my deliverer, my shield, in whom I take refuge, who subdues the peoples under me. O Lord, what are human beings that you regard them, or mortals that you think of them? They are like a breath; their days are like a passing shadow. Bow your heavens, O Lord, and come down; touch the mountains so that they smoke. Make the lightning flash and scatter them; send out your arrows and rout them. Stretch out your hand from on high; set me free and rescue me from the mighty waters, from the hand of aliens, whose mouths speak lies, and whose right hands are false. I will sing a new song to you, O God; upon a ten-stringed harp I will play to you. (Psalm 144:1–9)

Reflection

'My rock, my fortress, my stronghold, my deliverer and my shield.' Psalm 144 offers us an extraordinary variety of names for God. What do we learn from using them? Firstly, we learn to let go of any anxiety we may have about getting prayer right.

God is genuinely God. And we use human words to describe to ourselves what that means. Any authority they have is derived or approximate. What authenticates them is their ability to find both God and us at the place of encounter where the bush burns and we are called into the divine presence. This far. And then, 'Come no closer.'

These particular names for God are all strong words. God the rock is found within nature, within created reality. That is one place where we may look for God with complete confidence. A rock is an image of changeless solidity and security. You can cling to the rock; you can hide yourself in its crevices. But equally you can gaze on it from a distance and enjoy the illusion of change, as light plays on its surface and then scurries away.

So too with the fortress. This is a place of security. Yet made by human hands and so subject to conquest. We can take God by storm. Beating on the divine gates with the full force of our emotions, clamouring to be allowed in. And God can take us by storm, battering at our hearts. A stronghold is subtly different again, because it is where you store your treasure. It becomes the centre of your focus, whatever the direction of your gaze. Is that why W. H. Auden's lines are so memorable? 'He was my North, my South, my East and West,/ My working week and my Sunday rest,/ My noon, my midnight, my talk, my song.' His image is about the compass, about time and sound and music, but it carries the same sense of focus. Such focused love is absolute.

'My deliverer, my shield.' The psalmist anticipates the intervention of a God who draws near to us in our pain and distress, a God whose care of us is matched to human need. 'Bow your heavens, O Lord, and come down.' The Christian Church reads this as a text about the incarnation, about the work of Jesus who came to save us from the 'mighty waters', even at the risk of losing his own life for our sake.

Prayer

Rock of ages, cleft for me,
Let me hide myself in thee;
Let the water and the blood,
From thy riven side which flowed,
Be of sin the double cure:
Cleanse me from its guilt and power.

Not the labours of my hands
Can fulfil thy law's demands:
Could my zeal no respite know,
Could my tears for ever flow,
All for sin could not atone:
Thou must save, and thou alone.

Nothing in my hand I bring:
Simply to thy cross I cling:
Naked, come to thee for dress:
Helpless, look to thee for grace:
Foul, I to the fountain fly:
Wash me, Saviour, or I die.

While I draw this fleeting breath,
When my eyes shall close in death,
When I soar through tracts unknown,
See thee on thy judgement throne:
Rock of ages, cleft for me,
Let me hide myself in thee.

                    Augustus Montague Toplady, 1740–78

Exercise

Think of some of the other scriptural names for God: 'The Lord
is my Shepherd' (Psalm 23:1); 'The Lord is my light and my
salvation; whom shall I fear?' (Psalm 27:1); 'As a mother
comforts her child, so I will comfort you; you shall be comforted
in Jerusalem' (Isaiah 66:13). Notice what you feel as you pray
with them.

Friday – Week One: Jesus the Bread who is Taken

The identity of Jesus, the divine Son of God, is revealed to us in a variety of names. Today we recall the Bread of Life, taken or chosen by God for the redemption of the world.

Scripture Reading

Jesus said to them, 'I am the bread of life. Whoever comes to me will never be hungry, and whoever believes in me will never be thirsty. But I said to you that you have seen me and yet do not believe. Everything that the Father gives me will come to me, and anyone who comes to me I will never drive away; for I have come down from heaven, not to do my own will, but the will of him who sent me. And this is the will of him who sent me, that I should lose nothing of all that he has given me, but raise it up on the last day. This is indeed the will of my Father, that all who see the Son and believe in him may have eternal life; and I will raise them up on the last day.' (John 6:35–40)

Reflection

The setting is Capernaum. Jesus has fed the crowd of five thousand; has walked on the waters of the Lake of Galilee; and is now teaching the crowd about true hunger and true bread. He reminds them of Moses and the manna which came in the wilderness as the Chosen People made their way to Mount Horeb, and then to the Promised Land: 'Very truly, I tell you, it was not Moses who gave you the bread from heaven, but it is my Father who gives you the true bread from heaven' (John 6:32).

Then he goes a step further: 'I am the bread of life.' All that God promised in that manna and in the choice of a people and of a land is realised in Jesus himself. Everything that had gone before was to be fulfilled in Jesus.

So what, in essence, had gone before? God had made himself known to his people. He had revealed his desire to be known and loved. He had made a covenant, given a Law, secured a land for his people. In each of these actions he had reinforced their sense of election. The chosen, the beloved people were given everything. And now, in the Father's relationship with Jesus, that love becomes particular again. God chooses a person, an individual, in order to reveal the destiny of everyone. What the life, death and resurrection of Jesus secures is the redemption of the world. God's focused love and choice of Jesus becomes a generalised choosing of everyone. We all feed on the bread of the promise.

In the final week of his life, Jesus shared a meal with his friends. The tradition tells us that at that meal he took bread, blessed it, broke it and gave it to his disciples. The four-fold action of Jesus at the Last Supper is not something he pulled out of the air on that occasion. It was something he had learnt as his own core identity. He too is the beloved of God, taken or chosen by God – and then blessed, broken and given for the salvation of the world. Fridays provide us with a good opportunity to reflect on the eucharistic identity of Jesus – and also on our own. For the pattern of his life will be replicated in ours too. Just as Jesus was the beloved of God, the bread of life taken and chosen by God, so too may we be.

Prayer

Low in adoration bending,
Now our hearts our God revere:
Faith her aid to sight is lending:
Though unseen, the Lord is near;
Ancient types and shadows ending,
Christ our Paschal Lamb is here.

Thomas Aquinas, 1225–74

Guide me, O thou great Jehovah,
Pilgrim through this barren land:
I am weak, but thou are mighty,
Hold me with thy powerful hand:
Bread of heaven,
Feed me now and evermore.

Open now, the crystal fountain
Whence the healing stream doth flow;
Let the fiery, cloudy pillar
Lead me all my journey through:
Strong deliverer,
Be Thou still my strength and shield.

When I reach the verge of Jordan
Bid my anxious fears subside:
Death of death and hell's destruction;
Land me safe on Canaan's side:
Songs and praises
I will ever give to thee.

William Williams, 1717–91

Exercise
You are the object of God's desire. God loves you and chooses you and fills you with graces and blessings. Say slowly: 'I am the beloved of God' and notice how you feel. Do it several times during the day and notice when it is hard to say it and when it is easier.

Saturday – Week One:
Turning to God

We turn to God and pray with Psalm 121.

Scripture Reading

> I lift up my cyes to the hills – from where will my help
> come?
> My help comes from the Lord, who made heaven and
> earth.
> He will not let your foot be moved; he who keeps you
> will not slumber.
> He who keeps Israel will neither slumber nor sleep.
> The Lord is your keeper; the Lord is your shade at your
> right hand.
> The sun shall not strike you by day, nor the moon by
> night.
> The Lord will keep you from all evil; he will keep your
> life.
> The Lord will keep your going out and your coming in
> from this time on and for evermore. (Psalm 121)

Reflection

This is a song of ascent. That means a song or psalm that the
people would sing as they made their way towards the holy city
of Jerusalem on pilgrimage. We use it today as a way of reflecting
on the first word of the Lord's prayer. With Jesus we pray 'Father'
and realise what a wealth of meaning that word carries for us. It
tells us that God desires to be known because communication

and love and desire are at the heart of God's very being. The life of God within the Blessed Trinity is disclosed to us as constant communion. We trivialise the word if we simply see it as an image of intimacy. For God is revealed in glory in the burning bush, at the Transfiguration of Jesus and in all sorts of prophetic and mystical visions. And in Jesus, God comes as our liberator, our saviour. The strong rock and fortress of our deepest desires. We stand on holy ground.

Saturdays are turning points. Our reflection moves on. We prepare ourselves to begin a new week. We prepare for new graces and insights and blessings. But equally we rest in what has gone before. We draw on the spiritual insights of the previous week and deepen them. With that in mind we pray the words of Psalm 121 and realise that we too are journeying towards Jerusalem. This is where the events of the final week of Jesus's life will be played out. This is where he will come to humiliation, betrayal and shame. This is where he will come to glory.

The psalm offers a vision of hope, but also of realism. We do need help. We need the protection of a God who neither slumbers nor sleeps, whose concern for us is endless, whose love does not falter. We can rest safely in the knowledge that God, revealed to us as Father, is constantly attentive to our need. In God we can rest secure.

Prayer

> I kneel to pray
> and know not what to say;
> I cannot tell
> what shall be ill or well.
> But as I look
> into thy face or book,
> I see a love
> from which I cannot move,
> And learn to rest in this.
> So would I pray
> only to have thy way

in everything, wise Lord and
King.
Grant me but grace
in all to give thee place:
To have thy will perfectly. Amen.

Medieval prayer

Father we praise thee, now the night is over;
Active and watchful, stand we all before thee;
Singing we offer prayer and meditation:
Thus we adore thee.

Monarch of all things, fit us for thy mansions;
Banish our weakness, health and wholeness sending;
Bring us to heaven, where thy saints united
Joy without ending.

All holy Father, Son and equal Spirit,
Trinity blessed, send us thy salvation:
Thine is the glory, gleaming and resounding
Through all creation.

Gregory the Great, 540–604

Eternal Father,
turn our hearts to you.
By seeking your kingdom and loving one another,
may we become a people who worship you in spirit and truth.
Grant this through Jesus Christ, your Son,
who lives and reigns with you and the Holy Spirit,
One God, for ever and ever, Amen.

Roman Missal

Exercise
Repeat the exercise you personally found most helpful this week.
Only do it more slowly and take time to enjoy it.

2nd Sunday –
So What is Holiness?

'Hallowed be your name.' God is holy. We come into the divine presence and pray. But what attitudes do we bring with us when we come to prayer?

Scripture Reading

He also told this parable to some who trusted in themselves that they were righteous and regarded others with contempt: 'Two men went up to the temple to pray, one a Pharisee and the other a tax collector. The Pharisee, standing by himself, was praying thus, "God, I thank you that I am not like other people: thieves, rogues, adulterers, or even like this tax collector. I fast twice a week; I give a tenth of all my income." But the tax collector, standing far off, would not even look up to heaven, but was beating his breast and saying, "God, be merciful to me, a sinner!" I tell you, this man went down to his home justified rather than the other; for all who exalt themselves will be humbled, but all who humble themselves will be exalted.' (Luke 18:9–14)

Reflection

'Two men went up to the temple.' Which one are you? That is a trick question. One which is set up by the words with which Luke prefaces this parable. It is addressed to people who trust in themselves and look down on other people. Immediately we say, 'Well, thank God that isn't me.' Which is another way of saying, 'God, I thank you that I am not like other people.'

Start again. 'Two men went up to the temple.' This is a parable about prayer. About going up to the temple, to the place of encounter with God. This is a parable about wanting to come close to the holiness of God which, for Jesus and his contemporaries, dwells in the Holy of Holies within the Temple in Jerusalem. 'Hallowed be your name,' goes the prayer of Jesus. God is holy; we are drawn to the holiness of God.

So, we turn to God to pray and are confronted by these two people who war inside us. The one who says, 'Look God, I try really hard. I fast twice a week,' (the Law only asked you to fast once a week); 'I give a tenth of all my income,' (the Law only tithed grain, oil and wine). And the one who says, 'I am worthless, help me.' Jesus knows about the dilemma which is at the heart of human living. We all wrestle with an absolute and crippling sense of unworthiness. Some of us do this by covering up the problem; some by talking about it. The parable tells us that covering up does not work and that being truthful does. Both the characters in it are deeply religious. They crave the love and presence of God, and make their way up to the Temple. The man who tells God how good he is, comes down from the Temple humbled. The man who tells God how bad he is, comes down from the Temple exalted.

And because we want to be exalted we repeat the prayer of the tax gatherer: 'God, be merciful to me, a sinner.' But then we are left feeling vaguely dissatisfied because there is something disembodied about our prayer.

If you picture this scene in your imagination, what do you see? An empty church with one well-scrubbed character at the front and another, shifty-looking one at the back? Or a busy throng of people milling about, where it is quite difficult to work out who is who? Temple worship is corporate worship. Collectively we bring our unworthiness to God. So the real sin is to differentiate yourself from the human condition and deny that you are like other people. And the further sin is then to persecute those bits of you that do not match up to this lie. The thief, rogue and adulterer within.

Temple worship is corporate worship for the tax gatherer too. If we feel disembodied when we pray his prayer, there is a solution. Let go of the desire to be exalted. Take your desire to be good, saved, justified to the foot of the cross. Because that is where you will discover that you are a sinner and that you are like other people. Luke uses a powerful image in this story. The tax collector, 'standing far off, would not even look up to heaven, but was beating his breast'. That is an expression which does not occur often in the rest of the Bible. The women who accompany Jesus on the road to Calvary demonstrate their grief in this way and then, in Luke 23:48, we read that, 'When all the crowds who had gathered there for this spectacle saw what had taken place, they returned home, beating their breasts.' The spectacle in question is the crucifixion and death of Jesus.

Jesus is exalted, lifted up when he dies on the cross. That is where justification comes from and that is the safest place in the world for sinners to go. The exalted body of Jesus is the new Temple where we can take our deepest desires, confident that we are both judged and redeemed.

Prayer
Hallowed be your name. Holy, holy, holy is the Lord of Hosts; the whole earth is full of your glory. My eyes will see the King, the Lord of Hosts. Father, the hour has come; glorify your Son so that the Son may glorify you. Have mercy on me, a sinner and bring me to the place of all blessing, the foot of the cross.

Exercise
Go for a ten-minute walk. For five minutes of it, be the Pharisee going up to the Temple to pray. Then turn round and make your way back again. This time be the tax collector as he returns home. Notice what you feel.

Monday – Week Two:
Meeting God

'Hallowed be your name.' God is holy and, because of the saving work of Jesus, so are we too.

Scripture Reading

Like obedient children, do not be conformed to the desires that you formerly had in ignorance. Instead, as he who called you is holy, be holy yourselves in all your conduct; for it is written, 'You shall be holy, for I am holy.' If you invoke as Father the one who judges all people impartially according to their deeds, live in reverent fear during the time of your exile. You know that you were ransomed from the futile ways inherited from your ancestors, not with perishable things like silver or gold, but with the precious blood of Christ, like that of a lamb without defect or blemish. He was destined before the foundation of the world, but was revealed at the end of the ages for your sake. Through him you have come to trust in God, who raised him from the dead and gave him glory, so that your faith and hope are set on God. (1 Peter 1:14–21)

Reflection

God is holy – and so are we. What is the holiness of God like? When we pray: 'Hallowed be your name,' what do we mean? Last week we prayed and reflected on the name of God. This week we call on the holiness of God, and do so in confidence and hope and trust. We come into the holy presence of God, knowing that we may praise him.

In his first letter, Peter reminds us that we have moved from ignorance to obedience. Ignorance meant being afraid of God and of the judgement of God. It meant that we could never take the risk of coming into the presence of God in love and trust, or of turning to God with the abandon of true love. For we felt that we had done wrong. This wrong did not have a particular name. It was a generalised sense of failure, of not matching up to the divine will and purpose for us. Whereas obedience means trusting God and the measured mercy of God. We will not be blamed for things we have not done; and what we have done has been forgiven through the saving work of Jesus. When we come into the presence of God we do so as people who are ransomed, healed, restored and forgiven. Redemption is made perfect in us.

The work of Jesus is done. Our task is to rest in this certainty and to come to God in total confidence, certain that we are known by God in the very core of our being and loved into life and the fullness of life, whatever we have done or failed to do. With the passion, death and resurrection of Jesus, God's love is revealed as our salvation.

Prayer

> Praise to the Holiest in the height,
> And in the depth be praise;
> In all his words most wonderful,
> Most sure in all his ways.
>
> O loving wisdom of our God!
> When all was sin and shame,
> A second Adam to the fight
> And to the rescue came.
>
> O wisest love! that flesh and blood,
> Which did in Adam fail,
> Should strive afresh against the foe,
> Should strive and should prevail;

And that a higher gift than grace
Should flesh and blood refine,
God's presence and his very self,
And essence all-divine.

O generous love! that he, who smote
In man for man the foe,
The double agony in man
For man should undergo;

And in the garden secretly,
And on the cross on high,
Should teach his brethren, and inspire
To suffer and to die.

Praise to the Holiest in the height,
And in the depth be praise;
In all his words most wonderful,
Most sure in all his ways.

John Henry Newman, 1801–90

Now may the God of peace, who brought back from the dead our Lord Jesus, the great shepherd of the sheep, by the blood of the eternal covenant, make you complete in everything good so that you may do his will, working among us that which is pleasing in his sight, through Jesus Christ, to whom be the glory forever and ever. Amen.

Hebrews 13:20–21

Exercise
Try to recall a moment in your life when you have felt that you were totally understood, and totally forgiven. Rest in this certainty. If you have never had it, ask for it from the depths of your being.

Tuesday – Week Two: Glorifying God

We turn to God in complete confidence and say, 'Hallowed be your name.'

Scripture Reading

Abide in me as I abide in you. Just as the branch cannot bear fruit by itself unless it abides in the vine, neither can you unless you abide in me. I am the vine, you are the branches. Those who abide in me and I in them bear much fruit, because apart from me you can do nothing. Whoever does not abide in me is thrown away like a branch and withers; such branches are gathered, thrown into the fire, and burned. If you abide in me, and my words abide in you, ask for whatever you wish, and it will be done for you. My Father is glorified by this, that you bear much fruit and become my disciples. As the Father has loved me, so I have loved you; abide in my love. If you keep my commandments, you will abide in my love, just as I have kept my Father's commandments and abide in his love. (John 15:4–10)

Reflection

Jesus uses a powerful image to describe what we will experience once we begin to abide in the certainty that we are saved. 'I am the vine, you are the branches,' he says. And if you have ever looked at a vine, you will be aware that the vine and its branches are one plant. They have no existence apart from each other.

This is what union with God looks like. It is about closeness and growth and fruitfulness. It is about core identity, about our very being, and our development as the beloved of God. It is about total freedom and total dependency. About grace and life and energy and love.

That is why our lives give glory to God when we become disciples of Jesus and bear much fruit. Our humanity is swept into relationship with God and we display the source of our deepest identity with our every word and gesture and deed. We mirror the divine image and likeness. And, because of the transformation which is realised in us, other people can look at us and know what God is like. They spot the vine in the abundant growth of the branches. They see the vine and are able to taste of its fruit.

The vine image reminds us of another important dimension to this experience. It takes place within time and over time. That is the meaning conveyed by Jesus's use of the word 'abide'. This word occurs eleven times in this short passage of Scripture. So the vine image comes to act as a kind of commentary on an earlier line in John's gospel. In the prologue, we learn what it was that Jesus did when first he came to abide with us. The entry of Jesus into time and his abiding within human reality is described by John like this: 'And the Word became flesh and lived among us, and we have seen his glory, the glory as of the Father's only son, full of grace and truth' (John 1:14). Abiding within our flesh, Jesus reveals his Father's glory. So may we too, if we abide in him.

Prayer

> Come, my Way, my Truth, my Life:
> Such a Way, as gives us breath;
> Such a Truth, as ends all strife;
> Such a Life, as killeth death.

Come, my Light, my Feast, my Strength:
Such a Light, as shows a feast;
Such a Feast, as mends in length;
Such a Strength, as makes his guest.

Come my Joy, my Love, my Heart:
Such a Joy, as none can move;
Such a Love, as none can part;
Such a Heart, as joys in love.

George Herbert, 1593–1633

Grant us, Lord, to know in weakness the strength of thy incarnation: in pain the triumph of thy passion; in poverty the riches of thy Godhead: in reproach the satisfaction of thy sympathy: in loneliness the comfort of thy continual presence: in difficulty the efficacy of thy intercession: in perplexity the guidance of thy wisdom; and by thy glorious death and resurrection bring us at last to the joy of seeing thee face to face. Amen.

Source unknown

May our knowledge of you become ever clearer, that we may know the depth of your blessings, the length of your promises, the height of your majesty, and the depth of your judgement.

Francis of Assisi, 1182–1226

Exercise
Say these words of Henry Francis Lyte very slowly:
Abide with me; fast falls the eventide;
The darkness deepens; Lord, with me abide;
When other helpers fail, and comforts flee,
Help of the helpless, O abide with me.

Wednesday – Week Two:
Being Receptive to God's Glory

Glory is God's gift to us; it casts out every anxiety and fear.

Scripture Reading

Humble yourselves therefore under the mighty hand of God, so that he may exalt you in due time. Cast all your anxiety on him, because he cares for you. Discipline yourselves, keep alert. Like a roaring lion your adversary the devil prowls around, looking for someone to devour. Resist him, steadfast in your faith, for you know that your brothers and sisters in all the world are undergoing the same kinds of suffering. And after you have suffered for a little while, the God of all grace, who has called you to his eternal glory in Christ, will himself restore, support, strengthen, and establish you. To him be the power forever and ever. Amen. (1 Peter 5:6–11)

Reflection

'Hallowed be your name,' we pray. This moves our focus away from ourselves towards God. Some of the anxiety we ordinarily feel is immediately shifted because we are able to experience God's care for us. What we are offered is a foretaste of heaven, where the God of all grace will 'restore, support, strengthen and establish' us.

In our everyday lives though, we wrestle with anxiety and insecurity. We slip in and out of belief in our own salvation. Is that why Peter uses the image of a lion to describe the forces that roar around unsettling us? For a lion, as a dangerous wild beast, is the ultimate enemy to any pastoral community. References to lions abound in the Scriptures – and they are usually about the danger they represent to sheep and lambs. True peace comes when, in Isaiah's words, 'The wolf shall live with the lamb, the leopard shall lie down with the kid, the calf and the lion and the fatling together, and a little child shall lead them' (Isaiah 11:6). The lion does not go away; but it is reconciled to its prey, rather than warring against it. This is what the coming of the kingdom of God achieves: true, deep, everlasting peace.

In the interim though, we live with stress. Peter speaks for the whole Christian tradition when he says, don't try to bear it alone. 'Humble yourself under the mighty hand of God.' Let God help you bear your burden. And then remember all the other people who are similarly burdened. 'You know that your brothers and sisters in all the world are undergoing the same kinds of suffering.' This is where sanity and balance lie. This is where we will experience the love of God in our own being.

So how are we to cast our care upon the Lord? There is a call to honesty here. If you name your anxiety, it loses some of its power over you; if you turn it into a prayer, then God can meet you where you really are – as opposed to where you feel you ought to be. With confession, salvation comes where it is most needed.

Prayer

Have mercy on me, O God, according to your steadfast love; according to your abundant mercy blot out my transgressions.

Wash me thoroughly from my iniquity, and cleanse me from my sin.

For I know my transgressions, and my sin is ever before me.

Against you, you alone, have I sinned, and done what is evil in your sight, so that you are justified in your sentence and blameless when you pass judgement.

Indeed, I was born guilty, a sinner when my mother conceived me.

You desire truth in the inward being; therefore teach me wisdom
in my secret heart.

Purge me with hyssop, and I shall be clean; wash me, and I
shall be whiter than snow.

Let me hear joy and gladness; let the bones that you have crushed
rejoice.

Hide your face from my sins, and blot out all my iniquities.

Create in me a clean heart, O God, and put a new and right
spirit within me. Do not cast me away from your presence,
and do not take your holy spirit from me.

Restore to me the joy of your salvation, and sustain in me a
willing spirit.

Then I will teach transgressors your ways, and sinners will return
to you.

Deliver me from bloodshed, O God, O God of my salvation,
and my tongue will sing aloud of your deliverance.

O Lord, open my lips, and my mouth will declare your praise.

For you have no delight in sacrifice; if I were to give a burnt
offering, you would not be pleased.

The sacrifice acceptable to God is a broken spirit; a broken and
contrite heart, O God, you will not despise.

Psalm 51

O God our Father, hear me, who am trembling in this darkness,
and stretch forth thy hand unto me; hold forth thy light before
me; recall me from my wanderings; and, thou being my guide,
may I be restored to myself and to thee. Amen.

Augustine, 354–430

Be sober, be vigilant, because your adversary the devil goeth
about as a roaring lion, seeking whom he may devour, whom
resist, steadfast in the faith.

The Office of Compline

May almighty God have mercy on us, forgive us our sins, and
bring us to everlasting life. Amen.

Shared Text of the Absolution

Exercise
What frightens you most? Turn your fear into a prayer. And then repeat these words: 'Have mercy on me, O God, according to your steadfast love. Hallowed be your name.'

Thursday – Week Two:
God Desires our Good

'Hallowed be your name.' The bounty of God is poured out upon us.

Scripture Reading

I ask not only on behalf of these, but also on behalf of those who will believe in me through their word, that they may all be one. As you, Father, are in me and I am in you, may they also be in us, so that the world may believe that you have sent me. The glory that you have given me I have given them, so that they may be one, as we are one, I in them and you in me, that they may become completely one, so that the world may know that you have sent me and have loved them even as you have loved me. Father, I desire that those also, whom you have given me, may be with me where I am, to see my glory, which you have given me because you loved me before the foundation of the world. Righteous Father, the world does not know you, but I know you; and these know that you have sent me. I made your name known to them, and I will make it known, so that the love with which you have loved me may be in them, and I in them. (John 17:20–26)

Reflection

How many versions of the Lord's Prayer are there in the Scriptures? Two obviously, one in Matthew and one in Luke.

The familiar one and the one with which we are praying now. So far so good. But if the Lord's Prayer is the model of all prayer, as Jesus suggested when he said, 'And when you pray, say "Our Father" ', then we should not be surprised to see it, or traces of it, elsewhere in the gospels as well. Today we find just such a passage in John's gospel. The whole of chapter 17 is a kind of meditation on what glorifying the Father and being glorified by the Father mean. In this sense it can be read as an elaborated or expanded version of the Lord's Prayer.

Jesus's life is a 'Lord's Prayer' *too*. Here he is gathered with his friends at table. This is the last supper he will share with them. He has washed their feet as a reminder of his desire to abide with them, to share their humanity to the full. He has experienced the presence of the lion in their midst: Judas the betrayer, who cannot lie down in the company of the other disciples, but who takes off into the night. And now Jesus turns to God in prayer. 'After Jesus had spoken these words, he looked up to heaven and said, "Father, the hour has come; glorify your Son so that the Son may glorify you" ' (John 17:1). 'Hallowed be your name.' Glory is in the air as Jesus prays that his friends may know that they are loved by God and called into unity thereby. That is the way in which the glory of God will shine forth, for the God of all grace will 'restore, support, strengthen and establish' us. God desires our good, and with the gift of love and faith comes glory. That is what forgiveness looks like; that is what community looks like. God wills my good, God wills our good. That will bring us to glory.

Prayer
Almighty Father,
whose Son was revealed in majesty
before he suffered death upon the cross:
give us faith to perceive his glory,
that we may be strengthened to suffer with him
and be changed into his likeness, from glory to glory;

who is alive and reigns with you and the Holy Spirit,
one God, now and forever. Amen.

Collect for Lent 4, ASB

Glorious things of thee are spoken,
Zion, city of our God;
He whose word cannot be broken
Formed thee for his own abode.
On the Rock of Ages founded,
Who can shake thy sure repose?
With salvation's walls surrounded,
Thou mayest smile at all thy foes.

See! The streams of living waters,
Springing from eternal love,
Well supply thy sons and daughters,
And all fear of want remove;
Who can faint, while such a river
Ever flows their thirst to assuage:
Grace which, like the Lord, the giver,
Never fails from age to age?

Saviour, since of Zion's city
I, through grace, a member am,
Let the world deride or pity,
I will glory in thy name.
Fading is the worldling's pleasure,
All his boasted pomp and show;
Solid joys and lasting treasure
None but Zion's children know.

John Newton, 1725–1807

Glory, glory, glory. Let me hear those words, Lord. Give me your grace in abundance, grace upon grace; glory unto glory. Help me believe that I may safely cast my cares on you and that your forgiveness is assured. Be my Saviour. Be my glory.

Exercise
Imagine Jesus washing your feet. Listen to what he says to you.

Friday – Week Two: Jesus the Bread who is Blessed

Jesus is the object of God's desire and blessing.

Scripture Reading
> No one can come to me unless drawn by the Father who
> sent me; and I will raise that person up on the last day.
> It is written in the prophets, 'And they shall all be taught
> by God.' Everyone who has heard and learned from the
> Father comes to me. Not that anyone has seen the Father
> except the one who is from God; he has seen the Father.
> Very truly, I tell you, whoever believes has eternal life.
> I am the bread of life. (John 6:44–48)

Reflection
The eucharistic identity of Jesus is established in the events of
his life, death and resurrection. He is the beloved of God, the
Son who is chosen by his Father for the redemption of the world.

Today we recall the suffering and death of Jesus. But we do
so in a context which enables us to draw profit and fruit from
our prayer and reflection. Simply to contemplate suffering is a
soul-destroying affair. Those of us who have experienced great
sorrow and tragedy know how painful it can be. What makes it
bearable is the hope of resurrection. So too with the sufferings
of Jesus. In a time of gift and of grace, they kindle new faith
and hope and charity in us. How do they do this? By having
us concentrate on the whole pattern of God's dealings with
Jesus. This is when his eucharistic identity begins to shine

through – as does our own. For just as he was chosen by God, so are we. And just as he was blessed by God, so are we.

Notice the pattern, though. In our own lives and in the behaviour of society around us, we notice the tendency people have to take and to use. To choose and then to chuck. We take and break. God, however, does something quite different. Jesus is taken and blessed before he is broken. He goes to suffering knowing that he is the beloved of God. And that identity has been reinforced in him by the experience of God's further blessing.

Jesus says, 'I am the bread of life.' Not the bread of destruction. Not the bread of affliction. But the bread which feeds and nourishes us because it is good for us. The whole bent of his ministry is to raise people up, to make them feel better about being themselves, to set them free. This is why the gospel is good news. It calls us to be more than what we presently are. It offers us the promise of glory.

When we pray 'Hallowed be thy name,' we pray in the certainty that God both chooses and blesses us. That is how we share in the bread of life.

Prayer
Almighty God,
who wonderfully created us in your own image
and yet more wonderfully restored us
through your Son Jesus Christ:
grant that, as he came to share in our humanity,
so we may share in the life of his divinity;
who is alive and reigns with you and the Holy Spirit
one God, now and forever, Amen.

> Collect for Sunday after Christmas Day, ASB

Place your mind before the mirror of eternity!
Place your soul in the brilliance of glory!
Place your heart in the figure of the divine substance!
And transform your whole being into the image of the Godhead
    itself

through contemplation!
So that you too may feel what his friends feel
as they taste the hidden sweetness
which God himself has reserved
from the beginning
for those who love him.

Clare of Assisi, 1193–1253

But now thus says the Lord, he who created you, O Jacob, he who formed you, O Israel: Do not fear, for I have redeemed you; I have called you by name, you are mine. When you pass through the waters, I will be with you; and through the rivers, they shall not overwhelm you; when you walk through fire you shall not be burned, and the flame shall not consume you. For I am the Lord your God, the Holy One of Israel, your Saviour. I give Egypt as your ransom, Ethiopia and Seba in exchange for you. Because you are precious in my sight, and honoured, and I love you, I give people in return for you, nations in exchange for your life. Do not fear, for I am with you; I will bring your offspring from the east, and from the west I will gather you; I will say to the north, 'Give them up,' and to the south, 'Do not withhold; bring my sons from far away and my daughters from the end of the earth – everyone who is called by my name, whom I created for my glory, whom I formed and made.'

Isaiah 43:1–7

As bread that is taken – and so shall I be;
As bread that is blessed – and so shall I be;
As bread that is broken – and so shall I be;
As bread that is given – and so shall I be;
So is Jesus for me.

Exercise

Next time you eat a piece of bread, take the time to feel it and smell it and enjoy tasting it. Recall the words of Jesus: 'I am the bread of life.'

Saturday – Week Two:
Resting in God's Love

Saturday, the day of rest, offers us the chance to rest in God's forgiving love.

Scripture Reading

> I give you thanks, O Lord, with my whole heart; before the gods I sing your praise;
>
> I bow down toward your holy temple and give thanks to your name for your steadfast love and your faithfulness; for you have exalted your name and your word above everything.
>
> On the day I called, you answered me, you increased my strength of soul.
>
> All the kings of the earth shall praise you, O Lord, for they have heard the words of your mouth.
>
> They shall sing of the ways of the Lord, for great is the glory of the Lord.
>
> For though the Lord is high, he regards the lowly; but the haughty he perceives from far away.
>
> Though I walk in the midst of trouble, you preserve me against the wrath of my enemies; you stretch out your hand, and your right hand delivers me.
>
> The Lord will fulfil his purpose for me; your steadfast love, O Lord, endures forever. Do not forsake the work of your hands. (Psalm 138)

Reflection

'I bow down toward your holy temple and give thanks to your name for your steadfast love and your faithfulness; for you have exalted your name and your word above everything.' That is the meaning of the words 'hallowed be your name'. Our praise and thanksgiving are centred on God; our focus is on God and on his holy temple or dwelling place. This brings us to Jesus, the dwelling place of God who abides with us in the saving mysteries of the incarnation and his life, death and resurrection. We are called to share in these mysteries. And that is where we derive our sense of glory, but equally of inadequacy. Yet the God who loves us into life, also loves us into the fullness of life. So Jesus comes, not to condemn, but to save. The path to glory is opened for us.

What does that all look like, lived in the reality of human life? The model of discipleship which Luke returns to again and again in his gospel is that represented by Mary the Mother of Jesus. 'For though the Lord is high, he regards the lowly; but the haughty he perceives from far away.' These words are echoed in Mary's Magnificat: 'He has brought down the powerful from their thrones, and lifted up the lowly' (Luke 1:52). Mary herself is one of the lowly, the Virgin Daughter of Zion, as the tradition calls her, a woman of faith and of desire.

And so we sing of the glory of the Lord, 'For great are the ways of the Lord.' Resting in the Lord, we discover what it is to be lowly and what it is to be exalted – not by our own efforts, but by our participation in God's glory.

Prayer

> Mary the Dawn, Christ the perfect Day.
> Mary the Gate, but Christ the heavenly Way.
> Mary the Root, but Christ the mystic Vine.
> Mary the Grape, but Christ the sacred Wine.
> Mary the Corn-Sheaf, Christ the Living Bread.
> Mary the Rose-Tree, Christ the Rose blood-red.
> Mary the Fount, but Christ the cleansing Flood.
> Mary the Chalice, but Christ the saving Blood.

Mary the Beacon, Christ the haven's Rest.
Mary the Mirror, Christ the Vision blest.

                                        Source unknown

> Jesu, the very thought of thee,
> With sweetness fills my breast;
> But sweeter far thy face to see,
> And in thy presence rest.
>
> Nor voice can sing, nor heart can frame,
> Nor can the memory find,
> A sweeter sound than thy blest Name,
> O Saviour of mankind.
>
> O hope of every contrite heart,
> O joy of all the meek,
> To those who fall, how kind thou art,
> How good to those who seek!
>
> But what to those who find? Ah! this
> Nor tongue nor pen can show:
> The love of Jesus, what it is
> None but his loved ones know.
>
> Jesu, our only joy be thou,
> As thou our prize wilt be;
> Jesu, be thou our glory now,
> And through eternity.

                    12th century, tr. Edward Caswall, 1814–78

Exercise

Read 'Mary the Dawn' slowly. Choose your favourite line and read it over again, substituting your name for that of Mary. Let yourself rest in the sense of your own place within God's plan. Pray other lines in the prayer the same way, and notice what you feel.

3rd Sunday –
How Does the Kingdom Come?

'Your kingdom come' we pray each time we say the Lord's Prayer. But what does that mean? Are the armies of heaven to march to our rescue? Today's reading gives a startlingly different answer to that question. It is a unique parable, given only in Mark's gospel.

Scripture Reading

> He also said, 'The kingdom of God is as if someone would scatter seed on the ground, and would sleep and rise night and day, and the seed would sprout and grow, he does not know how. The earth produces of itself, first the blade, then the ear, then the full grain in the ear. But when the grain is ripe, at once he goes in with his sickle, because the harvest has come.' (Mark 4:26–29)

Reflection

'The earth produces of itself.' This is a story about the extraordinary abundance of God. God the giver of every gift asks of us simply that we be alive to the possibility of the kingdom: that we sow appropriately at the right season, and that we harvest when the time is ripe. As T. S. Eliot put it, 'I say to you: *Make perfect your will.* / I say: take no thought for the harvest, but only of proper sowing.' The growth of the kingdom is within the dispensation of grace. It will be given. We do not have to agonise over it.

Over the past thirty years, an enormous amount of ink has

spilled onto paper as people have outlined their plans for bringing about a kingdom of justice and peace. Liberation theology has brought hope to millions. It is based on the sense that the kingdom of God is for here and now. Within this dispensation of time, people have the right to hope for great things; heaven is not simply for when you are dead. With the approach of the millennium, another sea change is taking place. We live with wars and rumours of wars, with dissent, instability, fragmentation. All of these can be taken as signs of the endtime and are being interpreted as such.

But life will go on in the year 2000 and beyond. So how are we to hold on to mental and spiritual equanimity when time and the meaning of time are being reinvented all around us? The words of Jesus offer hope. Beyond all our campaigning, beyond all our anxiety, the kingdom of God is coming into being, sprouting and growing, we know not how. This parable urges on us a sense of passivity and receptivity in the presence of God's gift. It says, 'Be still, my soul.' Or, in the words of Psalm 37:7, 'Be still before the Lord, and wait patiently for him; do not fret over those who prosper in their way, over those who carry out evil devices.'

There is a message here about creation too. Nature is not hostile or precarious or our enemy or our victim. God's creation is energised from within. And so may we be too if we follow the message of this little parable. We pray for that sense of security which goes with interior freedom: 'Be still, my soul;' 'Your kingdom come.' We pray to know the moment, to be people who know when to sow and when to reap, because we are recollected and free to hear the call of the King.

Prayer

> Come, ye thankful people, come,
> raise the song of harvest-home!
> All is safely gathered in,
> ere the winter storms begin:
> God, our Maker, doth provide
> for our wants to be supplied;
> Come to God's own temple, come,
> raise the song of harvest-home!
>
> All the world is God's own field,
> fruit unto his praise to yield,
> wheat and tares together sown,
> unto joy and sorrow grown:
> first the blade, and then the ear,
> then the full corn shall appear;
> grant, O harvest Lord, that we
> wholesome grain and pure may be.
>
> Even so, Lord, quickly come
> to thy final harvest-home;
> from thy field upon that day
> all offences purge away;
> gather thou thy people in,
> free from sorrow, free from sin,
> there for ever purified,
> in thy glory to abide.

Henry Alford, 1810–71

Almighty God,
your Son has opened for us
a new and living way into your presence.
Give us pure hearts and steadfast wills
to worship you in spirit and in truth;
through the same Jesus Christ our Lord.

Collect for Pentecost 20, ASB

Exercise

Next time you are in a supermarket or at your corner shops, look at the fruit and vegetables on display there, and count how many different colours you can see arrayed before you. Next time you eat an orange or an apple, count the seeds in your hand. When you do this exercise, notice that God does not date stamp anything with 'meltdown 2000' or similar messages. And once again, notice what you feel.

Monday – Week Three:
What is the Kingdom of God?

'Your kingdom come.' As we pray these words of Jesus, what do we mean by them?

Scripture Reading

He put before them another parable: 'The kingdom of heaven may be compared to someone who sowed good seed in his field; but while everybody was asleep, an enemy came and sowed weeds among the wheat, and then went away. So when the plants came up and bore grain, then the weeds appeared as well. And the slaves of the householder came and said to him, "Master, did you not sow good seed in your field? Where, then, did these weeds come from?" He answered, "An enemy has done this." The slaves said to him, "Then do you want us to go and gather them?" But he replied, "No; for in gathering the weeds you would uproot the wheat along with them. Let both of them grow together until the harvest; and at harvest time I will tell the reapers, Collect the weeds first and bind them in bundles to be burned, but gather the wheat into my barn." ' (Matthew 13:24–30)

Reflection

Another seed parable. And one about people this time. Because in essence, the kingdom of God is about our openness to God, who is depicted in this parable as the householder. The sower sows seed in total good faith. Indeed Jesus is at pains to tell us that the very seed itself is good. But then along comes an enemy, someone who wants to wreck the life of the good seed by sowing weeds. What is the householder's reaction? Rather a philosophical one. Any attempt to uproot the weeds will destroy the chances of the young seedlings. So leave them be. The harvesting will happen in due course. And all shall be well.

In the interim, though, weeds and seeds make their way together towards the harvest. This is a parable about people and about the kingdom. How reassuring to find that the kingdom is not restricted to the pure or to an elite. That good and bad can co-exist and muddle along together. That the final judgement about what is a weed and what is not lies in the hands of a sane and sensible householder. We most likely have both inside ourselves.

So the kingdom is not about being set apart from other people. Nor is it about being set aside from ordinary human wilfulness and the rough and tumble of everyday living. That means that the kingdom is for people like us and not for people unlike us. When the harvest comes we will be a little clearer about some of the mess we presently inhabit. But right now, God protects us from our own tendency to tear up and root out and make ourselves holy and pure and good. All is gift. We are good seed. And all shall be well. The harvesting is in other hands, the hands of the householder-king.

Prayer

> I learned that love was our Lord's meaning.
> And I saw for certain, both here and elsewhere,
> that before ever he made us, God loved us;
> and that his love has never slackened,
> nor ever shall.
> In this love all his works have been done,
> and in this love he has made everything serve us;
> and in this love our life is everlasting.
> Our beginning was when we were made,
> but the love in which he made us
> never had beginning.

In it we have our beginning.
All this we shall see in God for ever.
May Jesus grant this.

Julian of Norwich, 1342–1416

The right hand of the Lord preserve me always to old age! The grace of Christ perpetually defend me from the enemy! Direct, Lord, my heart into the way of peace. Lord God, haste thee to deliver me, make haste to help me, O Lord.

Aethelwold, 908–84

Almighty God,
in Christ you make all things new.
Transform the poverty of our nature
    by the riches of your grace,
and in the renewal of our lives
make known your heavenly glory;
through Jesus Christ our Lord.

Collect for Epiphany 4, ASB

Rule in our hearts with your grace, that we may become fit subjects for your kingdom. We desire nothing more than to dwell in your kingdom, where we can watch you on your throne, and enjoy your perfect love. Amen.

Francis of Assisi, 1182–1226

Exercise

There are many different images of the kingdom of God. When you pray, 'Your kingdom come,' are you thinking about the future promise of heaven, about the coming of justice and peace on earth, about the openness of human hearts to God in the here and now – or a mixture of all three, and maybe about something else again? Ask God to bless each of these understandings and pray again, 'Your kingdom come.'

Tuesday – Week Three:
Where is the Kingdom of God?

Where is God's kingdom to come? How are we to recognise its coming?

Scripture Reading

One of the scribes came near and heard them disputing with one another, and seeing that he answered them well, he asked him, 'Which commandment is the first of all?' Jesus answered, 'The first is, "Hear, O Israel: the Lord our God, the Lord is one; you shall love the Lord your God with all your heart, and with all your soul, and with all your mind, and with all your strength." The second is this, "You shall love your neighbour as yourself." There is no other commandment greater than these.' Then the scribe said to him, 'You are right, Teacher; you have truly said that "he is one, and besides him there is no other"; and "to love him with all the heart, and with all the understanding, and with all the strength", and "to love one's neighbour as oneself", – this is much more important than all whole burnt offerings and sacrifices.' When Jesus saw that he answered wisely, he said to him, 'You are not far from the kingdom of God.' After that no one dared to ask him any question. (Mark 12:28–34)

Reflection

'You are not far from the kingdom of God.' This is the answer Jesus gives to someone who is intrigued by religious dispute and who wants to get at the heart of God's message. We know nothing about the scribe's personal life; all we do know is that Jesus commends him for his wisdom.

The dispute in question was triggered by a question from the Sadducees. They wanted to trick Jesus with a question which made a mockery of the idea of resurrection or life after death. Our scribe was impressed with Jesus's answer. He commends Jesus for his good answer, one which reminded his questioners that the God of the burning bush, the God of Abraham, Isaac and Jacob, is the God of the living. We mock God when we turn him into a God of the dead.

The scribe has a further question: 'Which is the greatest commandment?' What is faith really about? What is the point of it all? What are we striving for? When we pray, 'Your kingdom come,' what are we praying for? Jesus's answer goes straight to the heart of our deepest concerns. The greatest commandment is about God; the only other commandment is about other people. Both commandments require the same thing of us: that we be loving people. The coming of the kingdom is based on the reign of love; on the triumph of selflessness over ambition and greed; on letting go of our own need for approval and finding ourselves in service and care for others. This is far more demanding than the burnt-offerings and blood sacrifices of propitiation demanded by formal cultic religion. But only in this way, through that leap of the heart towards God and towards the service of other people, will the kingdom of God come. No wonder Jesus commended the scribe for his wisdom. This short conversation drives us to the heart of the gospel, to the heart of every religious search.

Prayer

King of glory, King of peace,
  I will love thee;
And that love may never cease,
  I will move thee.
Thou hast granted my request,
  Thou hast heard me;
Thou didst note my working breast;
  Thou hast spared me.

Wherefore with my utmost art
  I will sing thee,
And the cream of all my heart
  I will bring thee.
Though my sins against me cried,
  Thou didst clear me;
And alone, when they replied,
  Thou didst hear me.

Seven whole days, not one in seven,
  I will praise thee;
In my heart, though not in heaven,
  I can raise thee.
Small it is, in this poor sort
  To enrol thee:
E'en eternity's too short
  To extol thee.

George Herbert, 1593–1632

Almighty and everlasting God,
increase in us your gift of faith;
that, forsaking what lies behind
and reaching out to that which is before,
we may run the way of your commandments
and win the crown of everlasting joy;
through Jesus Christ our Lord.

Collect for Pentecost 19, ASB

Exercise
The scribe's question triggers a conversation with Jesus. What question do you want to ask him? Ask it, and pray to be attentive to his reply.

Wednesday – Week Three:
Christ the King

Christ is the King of glory, King of peace. In his kingdom we have redemption.

Scripture Reading

For this reason, since the day we heard it, we have not ceased praying for you and asking that you may be filled with the knowledge of God's will in all spiritual wisdom and understanding, so that you may lead lives worthy of the Lord, fully pleasing to him, as you bear fruit in every good work and as you grow in the knowledge of God. May you be made strong with all the strength that comes from his glorious power, and may you be prepared to endure everything with patience, while joyfully giving thanks to the Father, who has enabled you to share in the inheritance of the saints in the light. He has rescued us from the power of darkness and transferred us into the kingdom of his beloved Son, in whom we have redemption, the forgiveness of sins. He is the image of the invisible God, the firstborn of all creation; for in him all things in heaven and on earth were created, things visible and invisible, whether thrones or dominions or rulers or powers – all things have been created through him and for him. (Colossians 1:9–16)

Reflection

Paul reminds the converts at Colossae that he prays for them constantly. He asks for them to be filled with wisdom and understanding so that they will grow in the knowledge of God. This is a timely message, for some people in this young Church were experimenting with spiritual disciplines to get a religious high by their own efforts. Paul is resolute: what matters is sharing in the inheritance of the saints and living in the light. God has rescued us from any disciplines or practices which smack of the powers of darkness. Instead we have been transferred into the kingdom of the beloved Son, our Redeemer.

What comes next in this text is a song of praise to the beloved Son. He is the image of the invisible God. When we look at Jesus, we learn what God is like. In recent years there has been something of a crisis of confidence in the image of Christ as King. Some people find the very word itself repellent. The sixteenth-century master of the spiritual life, Ignatius of Loyola, used an exercise to help people over this hump. It is not the kind of thing Paul condemns in the Colossians, meaning it is not about strange practices or strange knowledge. Rather he had a very simple idea. If you want to know what Christ the King is like, think about the greatest leader you have ever known and respected. Who has been your mentor or role model? Whose style of leadership do you find inspiring? These are important questions because they help us get at a deep spiritual truth. That person, your own role model, the leader you admire, is an image to you of the invisible Christ, just as Jesus was of the invisible God. In this way we retrieve an image from the Christian tradition. In this way we learn to pray 'Your kingdom come' with even more conviction.

Prayer

Grant we beseech thee, O Lord, that by the observance of this
Lent we may advance in the knowledge of the mystery of Christ,
and show forth his mind in conduct worthy of our calling;
through Jesus Christ our Lord. Amen.

                              Gelasian Sacramentary, 8th century

Let folly praise what fancy loves,
I praise and love that Child,
Whose heart no thought, whose tongue no word,
Whose hand no deed defiled.
I praise him most, I love him best,
All praise and love is his;
While him I love, in him I live,
And cannot live amiss.

Love's sweetest mark, laud's highest theme,
Man's most desirèd light,
To love him, life, to leave him, death,
To live in him, delight.
He mine by gift, I his by debt,
Thus each to other due,
First friend he was, best friend he is,
All times will find him truc.

Though young, yet wise, though small, yet
strong,
Though Man, yet God he is;
As wise he knows, as strong he can,
As God he loves to bless.
His knowledge rules, his strength defends,
His love doth cherish all;
His birth our joy, his life our light,
His death our end of thrall.

                              Robert Southwell SJ, 1561–95

Exercise

Try Ignatius of Loyola's exercise for yourself. You might come up with an image of kingship as unexpected as the childhood friend described above by the Jesuit, Robert Southwell. Enjoy thinking about the qualities you most admire in the leader you choose. Then pray to Christ the King with new wisdom and understanding.

Thursday – Week Three:
The Call of the King

Christ calls us to serve with him.

Scripture Reading

Now after John was arrested, Jesus came to Galilee, proclaiming the good news of God, and saying, 'The time is fulfilled, and the kingdom of God has come near; repent, and believe in the good news.' As Jesus passed along the Sea of Galilee, he saw Simon and his brother Andrew casting a net into the sea – for they were fishermen. And Jesus said to them, 'Follow me and I will make you fish for people.' And immediately they left their nets and followed him. As he went a little farther, he saw James son of Zebedee and his brother John, who were in their boat mending the nets. Immediately he called them; and they left their father Zebedee in the boat with the hired men, and followed him. (Mark 1:14–20)

Reflection

Jesus comes to Galilee and begins to proclaim the gospel: 'the kingdom of God has come near, repent, and believe in the good news'. This call is addressed to everyone. But he then goes to the Sea of Galilee and calls Simon and Andrew even more directly. 'Follow me,' he says. These are the words which form the core of our reflection today. Jesus calls us to the intimacy of discipleship, to follow him absolutely and utterly. And with the call comes a promise: I will make you more than what you presently are. When we follow Jesus, we realise God's deepest desires for us. Our hearts begin to burn.

Can you remember what you prayed for on Ash Wednesday this year? Can you name the three graces you wrote down that day? These are the graces Jesus gives you and releases in you when you begin to follow him. You go towards fulfilment when you hear the call of the King.

Significantly, Simon and Andrew were not in church or visiting the poor when they were called. They were neither praying nor doing good works. Like James and John, they were getting on with their everyday tasks. God calls us in the midst of our daily lives; that is where we will be surprised by grace and called to glory. The grace is the gift of following Jesus; the glory is the glory of service.

Following Jesus is a gift. Mark tells us that Simon and Andrew jumped at the chance. They left their nets 'immediately', a word which Mark uses twenty-seven times in his gospel (John uses it twice, which suggests a quite different approach). You can see them bouncing into action, lit up by the desire to be with Jesus. 'Follow me.' Those words will take them to the foot of the cross, to the empty tomb. They will take them on an inner journey too. To the place where all our striving is laid aside and we learn to rest in the Lord and know him as our Saviour.

Prayer

> O thou who camest from above
> The pure celestial fire to impart,
> Kindle a flame of sacred love
> On the mean altar of my heart!
>
> There let it for thy glory burn
> With inextinguishable blaze,
> And trembling to its source return,
> In humble love and fervent praise.

Jesus, confirm my heart's desire
To work, and speak, and think for thee;
Still let me guard the holy fire,
And still stir up thy gift in me.

Still let me prove thy perfect will,
My acts of faith and love repeat,
Till death thy endless mercies seal,
And make the sacrifice complete.

Charles Wesley, 1707–88

Almighty God,
by whose grace alone we are accepted
and called to your service:
strengthen us by your Holy Spirit
and make us worthy of our calling;
through Jesus Christ our Lord.

Collect for Epiphany 2, ASB

I will pray for the grace I desire. Here it will be to ask of our
Lord the grace not to be deaf to his call, but prompt and diligent
to accomplish his most holy will.

Ignatius of Loyola, 1491–1556

Exercise
Repeat these words slowly:

Jesus, confirm my heart's desire
To work, and speak, and think for thee;
Still let me guard the holy fire,
And still stir up thy gift in me.

Thank God for the gift of your own calling, and say once more,
'Your kingdom come.'

Friday – Week Three:
Answering the Call of the King

Jesus does not simply call us; he gives us a task. We are to make his kingdom come.

Scripture Reading

In the sixth month the angel Gabriel was sent by God to a town in Galilee called Nazareth to a virgin engaged to a man whose name was Joseph, of the house of David. The virgin's name was Mary. And he came to her and said, 'Greetings, favoured one! The Lord is with you.' But she was much perplexed by his words and pondered what sort of greeting this might be. The angel said to her, 'Do not be afraid, Mary, for you have found favour with God. And now, you will conceive in your womb and bear a son, and you will name him Jesus. He will be great, and will be called the Son of the Most High, and the Lord God will give to him the throne of his ancestor David. He will reign over the house of Jacob forever, and of his kingdom there will be no end.' Mary said to the angel, 'How can this be, since I am a virgin?' The angel said to her, 'The Holy Spirit will come upon you, and the power of the Most High will overshadow you; therefore the child to be born will be holy; he will be called Son of God. And now, your relative Elizabeth in her old age has also conceived a son; and this is the sixth month for her who was said to be barren. For nothing will be impossible with God.' Then Mary said,

'Here am I, the servant of the Lord; let it be with me according to your word.' Then the angel departed from her. (Luke 1:26–38)

Reflection

This is a story about the coming of the kingdom. We usually read it on 25 March, the Feast of the Annunciation, or think about it on Mothering Sunday. But to confine it simply to a logical date in the calendar is to restrict its meaning. For this is a story for every day: it is about call and response and the coming of the kingdom. Gabriel bears God's message to Mary. He is her burning bush.

Mary will conceive and bear a son. The image of conception is like that of the seed growing in season. This is God's work and it will happen within time and within human reality. But it requires generosity from Mary and so God calls for her help in realising the divine plan. So she asks a question: 'How can this be?' This is the measured response of someone who wants to do God's will. What follows is an extraordinary sentence. The Holy Spirit will overshadow Mary, the power of the Most High, and she will bear a holy son, the Son of God.

This story tells us about God – the Blessed Trinity – and God's desire for the kingdom to come. It tells us about Mary and her intelligent, generous response. It tells us that God's plan and our own deep desires can meet. This is what we mean when we say that Jesus came to save us from our sins. That happened once, at the incarnation and at the cross, and it happens again, every day. Here, now. Every time we pray, 'Your kingdom come.' Put simply, it is the certainty that God loves us and wills our good. The story of Mary and the Angel Gabriel teaches us that God works very directly with people; that every invitation to help bring the kingdom into being is accompanied by the gift of grace: that therein lies our glory.

Prayer

I am no longer my own, but thine.
Put me to do what thou wilt, rank me with whom thou wilt:
Put me to doing: put me to suffering:
Let me be employed for thee, or laid aside for thee:
Exalted for thee, or brought low for thee:
Let me be full, let me be empty:
Let me have all things: let me have nothing:
I freely and heartily yield all things to thy pleasure and disposal.
And now, O glorious and blessed God, Father, Son and Holy
   Spirit,
Thou art mine and I am thine. So be it.
And the covenant which I have made on earth let it be ratified
   in heaven.

Methodist Covenant Service

Heavenly Father,
who chose the Virgin Mary, full of grace,
to be the mother of our Lord and Saviour:
fill us with your grace,
that in all things we may accept your holy will
and with her rejoice in your salvation;
through Jesus Christ our Lord. Amen.

Collect for Advent 4, ASB

Pour your grace into our hearts, O Lord,
that as we have known the incarnation
of your Son, Jesus Christ,
by the message of an angel,
so by his cross and passion
we may be brought to the glory of his resurrection;
through Jesus Christ our Lord. Amen.

Roman Missal

Exercise

Imagine God overshadowing you with the power of the Holy
Spirit and sending Jesus, his kingdom, to come right into your
heart. Listen, and say, with Mary, 'Let it be done to me according
to your word.'

Saturday – Week Three: Resting in God's Fidelity

'Father, hallowed be your name. Your kingdom come.'

Scripture Reading

> The Lord is my light and my salvation; whom shall I
> fear? The Lord is the stronghold of my life; of whom
> shall I be afraid?
>
> When evildoers assail me to devour my flesh – my
> adversaries and foes – they shall stumble and fall.
>
> Though an army encamp against me, my heart shall
> not fear; though war rise up against me, yet I will be
> confident.
>
> One thing I asked of the Lord, that will I seek after: to
> live in the house of the Lord all the days of my life,
> to behold the beauty of the Lord, and to inquire in
> his temple.
>
> For he will hide me in his shelter in the day of trouble;
> he will conceal me under the cover of his tent; he
> will set me high on a rock.
>
> Now my head is lifted up above my enemies all around
> me, and I will offer in his tent sacrifices with shouts
> of joy; I will sing and make melody to the Lord.
> (Psalm 27:1–6)

Reflection

Jesus *is* the kingdom of God. When he appears in Galilee, he
says, 'The time is fulfilled and the kingdom of God has come

near.' Today we rest in the knowledge and certainty that God is with us. In the gift of Jesus to the world he has pitched his tent among us.

If you look up into the roof of a Bedouin tent, you see a surprising sight. From the outside the tent looks impregnable. But once you are inside you realise that its thick black cloth is broadly woven and that it lets in pinpoints of light. When you look at it you have a sense that you are gazing up into the very heavens on a dark, dark night. You see an image of stars and galaxies stretching towards eternity. Living in the house of the Lord is like that. It is about comfort and security and safety, but also it is about having a window on eternity.

When you 'live in the house of the Lord', when the Lord is your light and salvation, then your perspective changes. So far we have concentrated on coming to this place. To the comfort and security and safety of our salvation, to the knowledge that God loves us utterly and unconditionally, whatever we do or fail to do; whatever we have done or failed to do. Indeed God loves us so much that he sends Jesus, his kingdom, to be our Saviour, to carry the burden of guilt or grief or anxiety that weighs us down.

Once we have rested in that certainty, then we must raise our eyes to the roof of the tent and find inspiration there. For from such a place of safety, our vision is renewed. And we can begin to contemplate the world through the eyes of God, that is to say with an eye on eternity.

The call of the King is a call to service. In the service of the King, we go forward into the fourth week of prayer, confident that he will use us to do God's will.

Prayer
Almighty God,
you have broken the tyranny of sin
and have sent the Spirit of your Son into our hearts
whereby we call you Father.
Give us grace to dedicate our freedom to your service,
that we and all creation may be brought

to the glorious liberty of the children of God;
through Jesus Christ our Lord, Amen.

Collect for Pentecost 4, ASB

> The spacious firmament on high,
> With all the blue ethereal sky,
> And spangled heavens, a shining frame,
> Their great original proclaim.
> The unwearied sun, from day to day,
> Does his Creator's power display;
> And publishes to every land
> The work of an almighty hand.
>
> Soon as the evening shades prevail,
> The moon takes up the wondrous tale,
> And nightly to the listening earth
> Repeats the story of her birth:
> Whilst all the stars that round her burn,
> And all the planets in their turn,
> Confirm the tidings, as they roll,
> And spread the truth from pole to pole.
>
> What though in solemn silence all
> Move round this dark terrestrial ball;
> What though no real voice or sound
> Amid their radiant orbs be found:
> In reason's ear they all rejoice,
> And utter forth a glorious voice,
> For ever singing as they shine:
> 'The hand that made us is divine!'

Joseph Addison, 1672–1719

Exercise
Practise resting today.

4th Sunday –
God Feeds Us All

'Give us each day our daily bread.' Jesus taught us all to pray that God would invite us daily to the great banquet.

Scripture Reading

He said also to the one who had invited him, 'When you give a luncheon or a dinner, do not invite your friends or your brothers or your relatives or rich neighbours, in case they may invite you in return, and you would be repaid. But when you give a banquet, invite the poor, the crippled, the lame, and the blind. And you will be blessed, because they cannot repay you, for you will be repaid at the resurrection of the righteous.'

One of the dinner guests, on hearing this, said to him, 'Blessed is anyone who will eat bread in the kingdom of God!'

Then Jesus said to him, 'Someone gave a great dinner and invited many. At the time for the dinner he sent his slave to say to those who had been invited, "Come; for everything is ready now." But they all alike began to make excuses. The first said to him, "I have bought a piece of land, and I must go out and see it; please accept my regrets." Another said, "I have bought five yoke of oxen, and I am going to try them out; please accept my regrets." Another said, "I have just been married, and therefore I cannot come." So the slave returned and reported this to his master. Then the owner of the house became angry and said to his slave, "Go out at once into the streets and lanes of the town and bring in the poor, the crippled, the blind, and the lame." And the slave said, "Sir, what you ordered has been done, and there is still room." Then the master said to the slave, "Go out into the roads and lanes, and compel people to come in, so that my house may be filled. For I tell you, none of those who were invited will taste my dinner." ' (Luke 14:12–24)

Reflection

Modern Scripture scholars suggest that Jesus came from a peasant community. This would be a community where people pray for two things: food and land. They are the basic currency of survival. Members of such a community live on the edge. They pray for daily bread, bread for today, and know that such bread is only earned by hard graft.

When we pray for daily bread, we are tempted to spiritualise our request and turn it into a nice polite prayer for grace, or for the Eucharist. That is what the man to whom Jesus told this parable did. 'Blessed is anyone who will eat bread in the kingdom of God!' he said. And so, to make him think even harder about his message, about its importance for now as well as for the coming kingdom, Jesus tells him a story. Someone gives a banquet and invites his friends. His own sort of people. When it comes to the day of the party, he has a major decision to make. What size animal should he kill? So he sends his slave out to check on the numbers. He is a generous, munificent host and wants to get it right. His guests are less gracious though. They tell transparent lies. After all, it is inconceivable that you should buy land or oxen without seeing them and trying them out. And the plea of marriage is ropy too, because our host would not have staged a banquet close to a wedding celebration.

The slave is sent out again. This time to find the 'crippled, the blind and the lame'. People who could not marry, or look at property or plough fields with oxen; people whom the Law impoverished by excluding them from society. Yet our host invites them to the banquet. And then, when there is still room, he has his slave go out and fetch in total strangers, compelling them to come to his table.

This is where the scope of the story extends to us. For the banquet which Jesus offers, the daily bread he wants to share with us is now within our reach. The children of the promise and of the Law did not come to the great dinner. Luke, the Graeco-Roman narrator of our gospel, is as much of a late arrival as most of us. He knows that we come to the feast with the poor, with the 'crippled, the blind and the lame', with people whom the Law excludes and consequently whom society rejects.

'Give us each day our daily bread.' Each day we pray to be reminded that we are needy and that God seeks our company at the great banquet. This is a deeply primitive need, like our need for food, like God's need for us. For the gracious, courteous host is the true hero of our story and he is gripped by his desire to bring us to his table and to feed us there.

Prayer
God of passion and desire, gracious host, call us to your table and share your friends with us. Give us our daily bread, meet our every need; give us the simplicity to know that we are crippled, blind and lame when we allow our own judgement to prevail over your gracious love, which is given to us in Jesus Christ our Lord, Amen.

Prevent, we beseech thee O Lord, our actions by thy holy inspirations and carry them on by thy gracious assistance, that every word and work of ours may be begun by thee and through thee be happily ended. Amen.

Roman Missal

Exercise
Close your eyes and imagine the host and his great banquet. Hear what he says as he welcomes you to it. Let him tell you how much he wants you to be there.

Monday – Week Four:
What Nourishes Us?

'Give us each day our daily bread.' What is the bread we pray for?

Scripture Reading

'Ask, and it will be given you; search, and you will find; knock, and the door will be opened for you. For everyone who asks receives, and everyone who searches finds, and for everyone who knocks, the door will be opened. Is there anyone among you who, if your child asks for bread, will give a stone? Or if the child asks for a fish, will give a snake? If you then, who are evil, know how to give good gifts to your children, how much more will your Father in heaven give good things to those who ask him!' (Matthew 7:7–11)

Reflection

Our Father in heaven desires to give good things to us. We have only to ask and to search and to knock. The focus of the Lord's Prayer changes at this point. We have named God, praised or hallowed God and prayed for the coming of our Saviour and his kingdom. Now we pray for ourselves and for our needs. 'Give us each day our daily bread': this is the prayer of people who know their need of something very basic and simple and sustaining. They are not laying up provisions for the next month, as though God were some giant superstore which you visit only occasionally and where you load up with supplies which are intended to last. When we pray the Lord's Prayer, we say we will live with a sense of need, and not seek to block it out. Each day we will come to God and ask and search and knock at the door. And each day we will receive and find and the door will be opened to us.

So what is the daily bread you seek? What nourishes you? And, more importantly, how do you discover it? The Christian spiritual tradition is not always helpful at this point. On the one hand, it says, 'Desire God and seek to do God's will' and on the other hand, it says, 'Be afraid of your own desires because they are likely to lead you astray.' The general confession in the Book of Common Prayer sums up the dilemma in a memorable way: 'Almighty and most merciful Father; We have erred and strayed from thy ways like lost sheep. We have followed too much the devices and desires of our own hearts.' 'Devices and desires' are treated as flashpoints of temptation, whereas they could be pathways between God and our very souls.

How can this be? Think once more about the words Ignatius of Loyola suggests we use when we pray: 'I pray for the grace I desire.' What do I most want today? Tolerance? Patience? Energy? Courage? Clarity? A sense of purpose? A sense of my own self-worth? Charity? Sticking power? If we know what we want, we can ask God for it and every time we say the Lord's Prayer, it will be given to us.

Prayer

Prayer is naught else but a yearning of the soul . . . when it is practised with the whole heart, it has great power. It makes a sour heart sweet, a sad heart merry, a poor heart rich, a foolish heart wise, a timid heart courageous, a sick heart well, a blind heart full of vision, a cold heart ardent. For it draws down the great God into the little heart; it drives the hungry soul up to the plenitude of God; it brings together these two lovers, God and the soul, in a wondrous place where they speak much of love.

Mechthild of Magdeburg, 1210–82

Almighty God,
who alone can bring order
to the unruly passions of sinful people:
give us grace,
to love what you command
and to desire what you promise,
that in all the changes and chances of this world,
our hearts may surely there be fixed
where lasting joys are to be found;
through Jesus Christ our Lord.

Collect for Easter 4, ASB

Soul of my Saviour, sanctify my breast,
Body of Christ, be thou my saving guest,
Blood of my Saviour, bathe me in thy tide,
Wash me with water flowing from thy side.

Strength and protection may thy passion be,
O blessed Jesus, hear and answer me;
Deep in thy wounds, Lord, hide and shelter me,
So shall I never, never part from thee.

Guard and defend me from the foe malign,
In death's dread moments make me only thine;
Call me and bid me come to thee on high
Where I may praise thee with thy saints for ay.

Latin, 14th century

Exercise

Find a big piece of paper. Sit down and breathe deeply to relax.
Then start to write a list of sentences that begin 'I want . . .'
Write quickly and don't censor yourself. Take as much time as
you need. When you have finished re-read the list and ask God
to help you understand what you have written.

Tuesday – Week Four:
Favourite Hymns

Singing or reading God's word helps us to know what we really value and desire.

Scripture Reading

As God's chosen ones, holy and beloved, clothe yourselves with compassion, kindness, humility, meekness,
and patience. Bear with one another and, if anyone has
a complaint against another, forgive each other; just as
the Lord has forgiven you, so you also must forgive.
Above all, clothe yourselves with love, which binds
everything together in perfect harmony. And let the
peace of Christ rule in your hearts, to which indeed
you were called in the one body. And be thankful.
Let the word of Christ dwell in you richly; teach
and admonish one another in all wisdom; and with
gratitude in your hearts sing psalms, hymns, and
spiritual songs to God. And whatever you do, in
word or deed, do everything in the name of the Lord
Jesus, giving thanks to God the Father through him.
(Colossians 3:12–17)

Reflection

'Sing psalms, hymns, and spiritual songs to God.' 'Let the word
of Christ dwell in you richly.' What is your favourite hymn?
This is a deeply important question. So take time to think about
the answer before you read the rest of this reflection.

Our favourite hymn tells us a great deal about our deep desires. It is as much of a revelation as writing an 'I want . . .' list. Notice what your favourite hymn tells you about God. How is God named in this hymn? Is he the 'Eternal Father, strong to save'? Is he the 'God of earth and altar'? And what about Jesus? Is he the 'Brightest and best of the sons of the morning'? Or the 'Servant King'? What happens in this hymn? Does it have a magnificent theological narrative like Wesley's 'And can it be?' Is it about freedom, about hope, about sin and redemption, about nature, about justice and the reign of God? Is it about peace, gentleness, serenity and calm? What does it tell you about your sense of community or Church, about where you feel comfortable and want to belong? What does it tell you about your 'daily bread', about what nourishes your spiritual life and growth?

Hymns are important for another reason too. Usually we sing them with other people. Even when we sing along with radio and TV hymns or with cassette hymns when we are driving, there is a corporate dimension to hymn singing which reminds us of the 'perfect harmony' for which we strive. In his letter to the Colossians, Paul reminds us that the call to enjoy the peace of Christ is a call to be one in Christ. This gives us a further insight into the meaning of the words 'Give us each day our daily bread.' After all, we do not pray 'Give me my daily bread.' Our deepest desires, and certainly our most spiritual ones – the ones which most clearly express our own personal search for meaning – will draw us in love towards other people.

Prayer

> And can it be that I should gain
> An interest in the Saviour's blood?
> Died he for me, who caused his pain?
> For me? Who him to death pursued?
> Amazing love! How can it be
> That thou, my God, shouldst die for me?

'Tis myst'ry all: th'Immortal dies!
Who can explore his strange design?
In vain the firstborn seraph tries
To sound the depths of love divine.
'Tis mercy all! Let earth adore!
Let angel minds inquire no more.

He left his Father's throne above
(So free, so infinite his grace!)
Emptied himself of all but love,
And bled for Adam's helpless race.
'Tis mercy all, immense and free,
For, O my God, it found out me!

Long my imprisoned spirit lay,
Fast bound in sin and nature's night.
Thine eye diffused a quick'ning ray;
I woke; the dungeon flamed with light,
My chains fell off, my heart was free,
I rose, went forth, and followed thee.

No condemnation now I dread,
Jesus, and all in him, is mine.
Alive in him, my living head,
And clothed in righteousness divine,
Bold I approach th'eternal throne,
And claim the crown, through Christ my own.

Charles Wesley, 1707–88

Blessed Lord, who caused all holy scriptures to be written for
    our learning:
help us so to hear them,
to read, mark, learn, and inwardly digest them,
that, through patience, and the comfort of your holy word,
we may embrace and for ever hold fast the hope of everlasting
    life,
which you have given us in our Saviour Jesus Christ.

Collect for Advent 2, ASB

Exercise
Next time you join in radio or TV worship, think about the other people who are listening or watching, and pray for them.

Wednesday – Week Four:
A Hungry World

'Give us each day our daily bread.' Whose daily bread?

Scripture Reading

> O Lord, how manifold are your works! In wisdom you
> have made them all; the earth is full of your creatures.
> Yonder is the sea, great and wide, creeping things in-
> numerable are there, living things both small and
> great.
> There go the ships, and Leviathan that you formed to
> sport in it.
> These all look to you to give them their food in due
> season; when you give to them, they gather it up;
> when you open your hand, they are filled with good
> things.
> When you hide your face, they are dismayed; when you
> take away their breath, they die and return to their
> dust.
> When you send forth your spirit, they are created; and
> you renew the face of the ground. (Psalm 104:24–30)

Reflection

The world forms an ecological whole. Each eco-system lives
within a dense series of relationships. This is the wisdom of our
age, a wisdom which inspires people to live with a new con-
sciousness about creation and about the human family. The older
wisdom of the Scriptures pushes the argument though. It says

that 'The earth is full of *your* creatures,' insisting that our primary relationship is with God and that everything else is derived from that.

This reminds us that concern about global community is older than we imagine. But why is it that this concern has emerged with such force in our own times? What is it about nowadays that makes us realise that when we talk about 'loving our neighbour as ourself', we actually encompass a far denser web of connections than would previously have been possible. The media help, of course. We now know what hidden bits of the planet and hidden peoples look like. We travel more. But there is another reason too. We are aware that we do not live in isolation from one another, that our behaviour affects other people, as well as the environment.

So how are we to pray 'Give us today our daily bread' when we know that many people in the world go hungry? Should we even be praying for ourselves, in the circumstances, or should we not rather be praying for them? We know that some people are hungry and some people have too much to eat. We also know that not all we eat is good for us. Our food chains are in disarray. Then there is a further issue. Our need for stimulation, for constant sound and images, for example, could be taken as a manifestation of a psychological over-stimulation. At some deep level we cannot allow ourselves to be hungry or to experience want and need. The very thought of it is terrifying.

If truth be told, this is precisely why we need to turn to God and pray 'Give us today our daily bread.' If we pray this over and over, we will lose our fear of hunger; we will be prepared to share the gifts of our abundant world more generously; we will stop living at the expense of other people and of the planet.

Prayer

Hildegard writes 'as' God or the Holy Spirit when she says:
'I am that supreme and fiery force that sends forth all the sparks of life. I am that living and fiery essence of the divine substance that flows in the beauty of the fields. I shine in the water, I burn in the sun and the moon and the stars. I am the force that lies

hid in the winds, from me they take their source, and as a man and woman may move because they breathe, so no fire burns but by my blast. All these live because I am in them and am of their life. I am wisdom. Mine is the blast of the thundered word by which all things were made. I permeate all things that they may not die. I am life.'

Hildegard of Bingen, 1098–1179

We plough the fields, and scatter
The good seed on the land,
But it is fed and watered
By God's almighty hand;
He sends the snow in winter
The warmth to swell the grain,
The breezes and the sunshine,
And soft refreshing rain:
All good gifts around us
Are sent from heaven above;
Then thank the Lord, O thank the Lord,
For all his love.

He only is the maker
Of all things near and far;
He paints the wayside flower,
He lights the evening star;
The winds and waves obey him,
By him the birds are fed;
Much more to us, his children,
He gives our daily bread:

We thank thee then, O Father,
For all things bright and good:
The seed-time and the harvest,
Our life, our health, our food.
Accept the gifts we offer
For all thy love imparts,
And, what thou most desirest,
Our humble, thankful hearts:

M. Claudius, 1740–1815

Exercise
Think about hunger, experience it if need be. Thank God as
you eat.

Thursday – Week Four: Who are our Table Companions?

As the beloved sons and daughters of God, we do not eat alone.

Scripture Reading

After this he went out and saw a tax collector named Levi, sitting at the tax booth; and he said to him, 'Follow me.' And he got up, left everything, and followed him. Then Levi gave a great banquet for him in his house; and there was a large crowd of tax collectors and others sitting at the table with them. The Pharisees and their scribes were complaining to his disciples, saying, 'Why do you eat and drink with tax collectors and sinners?' Jesus answered, 'Those who are well have no need of a physician, but those who are sick; I have come to call not the righteous but sinners to repentance.' (Luke 5:27–32)

Reflection

When you invite Jesus into your house, he gets to meet your friends. That was Levi's experience; it can be ours, too, if we are prepared to let it be. Levi was a tax collector, that is to say someone who collaborated with the system of occupation. He gathered taxes on behalf of the Romans which means that his ritual and religious purity were questionable, as well as his morals. But here was a generous man. When Jesus called him to be a follower, his instinctive reaction was to give a party. And everyone came. No excuses on this occasion.

Are sinners more generous than saints? The answer is not straightforward. When we pray 'Give us each day our daily bread,' we pray to imitate the generosity of God and the gift of Jesus. We pray to lose our fear and our inhibitions. We pray to widen the scope of our own hospitality, to bring others to the promise which we enjoy.

This story is not set in any particular location. We do not know where Levi lived. But at the beginning of this chapter in Luke's gospel, the site is identified in another way: 'Once while Jesus was standing beside the lake of Gennesaret, and the crowd was pressing in on him *to hear the word of God . . .*' (Luke 5:1). Jesus is the Word of God. We press in on him to hear God speak. Levi was among the listeners who heard the word of God. We learn nothing further about him in Luke's gospel, unless he is listed as Matthew in Luke 6:15 where the apostles are identified by name. What counts is the moment when Jesus calls him and he answers by rising up, following, and giving a party to bring his friends to the Word.

When we rise up and follow the Lord, who do we bring with us? Who are our friends? Who enjoys access to the Word because of us? Are there any friends we would be ashamed to bring to the banquet? Why? Would Jesus not enjoy their company – and they his?

At its most generous, the Church mirrors the experience of Levi for us. It calls us to the simple practice of community and communion. In worship it offers us the possibility of mixing with sinners, with other people who are like us because their humanity too is wounded; it brings us to communion also, to the eucharistic bread.

Prayer

> Jesus, we thus obey
> Thy last and kindest word;
> Here, in thine own appointed way,
> We come to meet thee, Lord.

Our hearts we open wide
To make our Saviour room;
And lo! The Lamb, the Crucified,
The sinners' friend, is come!

His presence makes the feast;
And now our presence feel
The glory not to be expressed,
The joy unspeakable.

With pure celestial bliss
He doth our spirits cheer;
His house of banqueting is this,
And he hath brought us here.

He bids us drink and eat
Imperishable food;
He gives his flesh to be our meat,
And bids us drink his blood.

Whate'er the Almighty can
To pardoned sinners give,
The fulness of our God made
man
We here with Christ receive.

                              Charles Wesley, 1707–88

Father of peace, we are joyful in your Word,
your Son Jesus Christ, who reconciles us to you.
Let us hasten toward Easter with the eagerness of faith and love.
We ask this through our Lord Jesus Christ, your Son,
who lives and reigns with you and the Holy Spirit, one God, for
ever and ever, Amen.

              Collect for 4th Sunday of Lent, Roman Missal

Exercise
Where do you experience community and communion most
fruitfully?

Friday – Week Four:
Jesus, the Bread who is Broken

The eucharistic identity of Jesus becomes more clearly defined.

Scripture Reading

I am the bread of life. Your ancestors ate the manna in the wilderness, and they died. This is the bread that comes down from heaven, so that one may eat of it and not die. I am the living bread that came down from heaven. Whoever eats of this bread will live forever; and the bread that I will give for the life of the world is my flesh. (John 6:48–51)

Reflection

Jesus is the bread of life, the living bread from heaven. How does his life get translated into our life? How are we to feed on him? The people who first heard these words asked the same question. John tells us that they asked, 'How can this man give us his flesh to eat?' They were embarrassed by what they heard him say, and puzzled as well.

We have the advantage of hindsight. We know that Jesus, the Word of God and living bread from heaven, was taken, blessed and broken in the saving mysteries of his life and death. In communion services, we in turn take, bless and break the bread and give thanks and praise to God. When we pray 'Give us each day our daily bread,' the words have a eucharistic overtone. But, as we have already seen, their meaning is not restricted to that, just as the life of Jesus was not restricted to the last meal he shared with his friends. Nor was his work of salvation restricted to his death on the cross, though that is where he was most profoundly broken. The breaking began when the Angel Gabriel came to Mary and God's glory broke through. Jesus was first chosen and blessed and now he will be broken.

Jesus is the living bread from heaven. How are we to feed on him? The reality is that bread has to be broken if we are to eat. The Christian mystical tradition has produced some of its most passionate writing on this theme. Here is a passage from the writings of Marguerite d'Oingt, a Carthusian prioress who was born in 1310: 'For are you not my mother and more than my mother? The mother who bore me laboured in delivering me for one day and one night but you, my sweet and lovely Lord, laboured for me for more than thirty years. Ah with what love you laboured for me and bore me through your whole life. But when the time approached for you to be delivered, your labour pains were so great that your holy sweat was like great drops of blood that came out from your body and fell on the earth. When the hour of your delivery came you were placed on the hard bed of the cross and your nerves and all your veins burst when in one day you gave birth to the whole world.'

Prayer

> My God, I love thee – not because
> I hope for heaven thereby,
> Nor yet because who love thee not
> Are lost eternally.
>
> Thou, O my Jesus, thou didst me
> Upon the cross embrace;
> For me didst bear the nails and spear,
> And manifold disgrace;
>
> And griefs and torments numberless,
> And sweat of agony,
> Yea, death itself, and all for one
> Who was thine enemy.

Then why, O blessed Jesus Christ,
Should I not love thee well?
Not for the sake of winning heaven,
Nor of escaping hell;

Not with the hope of gaining aught,
Nor seeking a reward;
But as thyself hast loved me,
O ever-loving Lord!

E'en so I love thee, and will love,
And in thy praise will sing;
Solely because thou art my God,
And my eternal King.

Francis Xavier, 1506–52

The Body of our Lord Jesus Christ which was given for thee, preserve thy body and soul unto everlasting life. Take and eat this in remembrance that Christ died for thee, and feed on him in thy heart by faith with thanksgiving.

The Blood of our Lord Jesus Christ, which was shed for thee, preserve thy body and soul unto everlasting life. Drink this in remembrance that Christ's Blood was shed for thee, and be thankful.

The Order of the Ministration of the Holy Communion, BCP

Exercise

'Feed on him in your hearts by faith with thanksgiving.' Say these words again slowly and consider Jesus who was taken, blessed and broken for you. Then repeat these words from the Lord's Prayer: 'Father, hallowed be your name. Your kingdom come. Give us each day our daily bread.'

Saturday – Week Four:
Feeding on the Bread of Life

What happens when our identity is modelled on that of Jesus?

Scripture Reading

> The Lord upholds all who are falling, and raises up all who are bowed down.
>
> The eyes of all look to you, and you give them their food in due season.
>
> You open your hand, satisfying the desire of every living thing.
>
> The Lord is just in all his ways, and kind in all his doings.
>
> The Lord is near to all who call on him, to all who call on him in truth.
>
> He fulfils the desire of all who fear him; he also hears their cry, and saves them.
>
> The Lord watches over all who love him, but all the wicked he will destroy.
>
> My mouth will speak the praise of the Lord, and all flesh will bless his holy name forever and ever.
> (Psalm 145:14–21)

Reflection

'The Lord upholds all who are falling.' However great our pain, however great our sense of loss, God is with us. Jesus is the bread of life. When we feed on him, we come to salvation. Today's psalm reflects on the experience of the Exodus. From the slavery of Egypt, the Chosen People were brought to the Promised Land. They went through the Red Sea; they spent forty years wandering around in confusion in the wilderness; they received the Law – and promptly began to break it; their memories began to play up as they heard siren voices calling to go backwards instead of forwards. This is symbolised most tellingly in the story of their complaint about food. God gave them manna in the wilderness; food from heaven as they called it. But what happened next?

The Book of Numbers tells how the Israelites began to complain: ' "We remember the fish we used to eat in Egypt for nothing, the cucumbers, the melons, the leeks, the onions, and the garlic; but now our strength is dried up, and there is nothing at all but this manna to look at." Now the manna was like coriander seed, and its colour was like the colour of gum resin. The people went around and gathered it, ground it in mills or beat it in mortars, then boiled it in pots and made cakes of it; and the taste of it was like the taste of cakes baked with oil. When the dew fell on the camp in the night, the manna would fall with it' (Numbers 11:5–9). Manna, God's great gift from heaven, proved a poor second to the gastronomic memories of foody life in Egypt, and when you read that description of it, you can see why.

This is a problem we recognise. For the journey we all make from captivity to freedom is littered with false starts and wanderings. And our memories do play tricks on us. We forget the full horror of slavery, and crave its delights. So what does the manna symbolise? Clearly, as food goes, it was boring. But the psalm calls it food in due season and reminds us that it comes from the hand of God. That is why we remember manna when we pray, 'Give us each day our daily bread.' We know that we need the gift of God and the constant daily assurance that in the saving events of the life and death of Jesus, we journey towards deep freedom and peace. That is to say, our salvation.

Prayer

Let all mortal flesh keep silence, and with fear and trembling
      stand;
Ponder nothing earthly-minded, for with blessing in his hand
Christ our God to earth descended, our full homage to demand.

King of kings, yet born of Mary, as of old on earth he stood,
Lord of lords, in human vesture – in the body and the blood –
He will give to all his faithful his own self for heavenly food.

Rank on rank the host of heaven spreads its vanguard on the
      way,
As the Light of light descendeth from the realms of endless
      day,
That the powers of hell may vanish as the darkness clears away.

At his feet the six-winged seraph; cherubim with sleepless eye
Veil their faces to the Presence, as with ceaseless voice they cry –
Alleluia, alleluia, alleluia, Lord most high!

> From the Liturgy of St James, tr. G. Moultrie, 1829–85

Almighty God,
we thank you for feeding us
with the body and blood of your Son Jesus Christ.
Through him we offer you our souls and bodies
to be a living sacrifice.
Send us out
in the power of your Spirit
to live and work
to your praise and glory. Amen.

> Order for Holy Communion, ASB

Here, dying for the world, the world's life hung,
Laving a world's sin in that deathly tide;
That downbent head raised earth above the
stars:
O timeless wonder! Life, because One died.

> Alcuin of York, 735–804

Exercise
Think back over the exercises you have done this week and repeat your favourite one, or repeat your favourite prayer.

5th Sunday –
God's Generosity and
Forgiveness

Why are we to forgive each other? Because God is merciful and forgives us totally and utterly and unconditionally.

Scripture Reading

Then Jesus said to the disciples, 'There was a rich man who had a manager, and charges were brought to him that this man was squandering his property. So he summoned him and said to him, "What is this that I hear about you? Give me an accounting of your management, because you cannot be my manager any longer." Then the manager said to himself, "What will I do, now that my master is taking the position away from me? I am not strong enough to dig, and I am ashamed to beg. I have decided what to do so that, when I am dismissed as manager, people may welcome me into their homes." So, summoning his master's debtors one by one, he asked the first, "How much do you owe my master?" He answered, "A hundred jugs of olive oil." He said to him, "Take your bill, sit down quickly, and make it fifty." Then he asked another, "And how much do you owe?" He replied, "A hundred containers of wheat." He said to him, "Take your bill and make it eighty." And his master commended the dishonest manager because he had acted shrewdly; for the children of this age are more shrewd in dealing with their own generation than are the children of light.' (Luke 16:1–8)

Reflection

This is a story about a community. Some of the characters are identified by name: the master and his agent, two of the master's debtors. Others feature indirectly: the people who bring charges against the agent. Jesus tells this parable to his disciples. It is one of those tricky stories where the meaning slithers around and we have the feeling that someone dishonest gets rewarded or at least commended, when our natural instinct is to want them to be punished.

So what is this story about and how does it work? The master is a benign and generous man. His estate manager or agent is a rogue. When the master gets to hear of this he acts with extraordinary generosity. Instead of having the agent thrown into prison, he asks him if the charges are true and, on getting no reply, simply dismisses him. The manager walks away a free man. But what about his place in the community? How can that be assured when he has no job? He does not want to dig or to beg, but he does want friends. That is when he calls in people who are indebted to his former master and starts writing off half their debts for them. The whole community stands to benefit from this sudden generosity. The rogue with the questionable reputation will have friends after all. But what about the master, what is his reaction?

He commends the manager for acting shrewdly, and we are left feeling uncomfortable. Surely justice requires that the manager be punished, that the master extract some kind of revenge? We put limits on forgiveness. But this is a story about the generous love of God. It is a story about a whole community and a dense network of relationships, which are affected both by sin and by forgiveness. That is why, in the Lord's Prayer, we are exhorted to pray, 'And forgive us our sins for we ourselves forgive those indebted to us.' Our need for forgiveness is absolute. God meets this need and exhorts us to become forgiving people ourselves.

Prayer

Happy are those whose transgression is forgiven, whose sin is
   covered.

Happy are those to whom the Lord imputes no iniquity, and in
   whose spirit there is no deceit.

While I kept silence, my body wasted away through my groaning
   all day long.

For day and night your hand was heavy upon me; my strength
   was dried up as by the heat of summer.

Then I acknowledged my sin to you, and I did not hide my
   iniquity; I said, 'I will confess my transgressions to the Lord,'
   and you forgave the guilt of my sin.

Therefore let all who are faithful offer prayer to you; at a time
   of distress, the rush of mighty waters shall not reach them.

You are a hiding place for me; you preserve me from trouble;
   you surround me with glad cries of deliverance . . .

Many are the torments of the wicked, but steadfast love
   surrounds those who trust in the Lord.

Be glad in the Lord and rejoice, O righteous, and shout for joy,
   all you upright in heart.

Psalm 32:1–7, 10–11

O God, who knowest us to be set
in the midst of so many and great dangers,
that by reason of the frailty of our nature
we cannot always stand upright:
grant to us such strength and protection
as may support us in all dangers
and carry us through all temptations;
through Jesus Christ our Lord, Amen.

Collect for Epiphany 4, BCP

Exercise

'Happy are those whose transgression is forgiven.' Reflect on
occasions when we have forced other people to pay over the
odds. Is there a kind of practical wisdom which requires us to
back down? What would the effects be?

Monday – Week Five:
Naming our Sins –
as Individuals

God is merciful and forgives us totally and utterly and unconditionally. That is why we can face up to our own sinfulness.

Scripture Reading

'Do not judge, so that you may not be judged. For with the judgement you make you will be judged, and the measure you give will be the measure you get. Why do you see the speck in your neighbour's eye, but do not notice the log in your own eye? Or how can you say to your neighbour, "Let me take the speck out of your eye," while the log is in your own eye? You hypocrite, first take the log out of your own eye, and then you will see clearly to take the speck out of your neighbour's eye.' (Matthew 7:1–5)

Reflection

Jesus asks us to take a long cool look at ourselves. This requires great courage, because what we will find is a log, that is to say something quite weighty which needs to be worked on before we see our neighbours clearly. When we do see them properly, we will of course be able to remove the maddening speck from their eye. But we will do so more kindly, for we will be wiser people ourselves.

That is the traditional reading of this story from the Sermon on the Mount. It makes perfect sense. It asks us to turn our gaze inwards and sort out our own mess before we start attacking other people. All well and good. But there is another dimension to this text which is so startlingly obvious that it sometimes passes us by. This is a story about relationships. We do not come to God alone. My neighbour is an integral part of my journey to God. How I treat my neighbour matters. It is not an add-on, an optional extra. We negotiate our identity within the everyday framework of the people we know and how we get on with them. We do not do this apart from them. Our attitude to people who are our unknown neighbours is important too. It is a measure of how happy we are to be loved by God, that we share our world and its resources with everyone else. It is a measure of how secure we feel in God's love, that we acknowledge that God makes and loves them too. These bits of our Christian identity do not live in separate boxes; they are deeply connected to each other. When you adjust one of them, the others move around as well.

The individual who accepts God's love and forgiveness is like a bright star, constellating with all the other stars and giving a new shape and pattern and order to the night sky. For this is a story about light as well, about that clarity which makes for truth, where beams and specks get cleared out of the way and everyone gets to see better. All vision is renewed.

So too with sin. It gets shifted and dispersed. In the Lord's Prayer in Luke's gospel we pray: 'And forgive us our sins since we ourselves forgive everyone indebted to us.' Jesus attributes open-heartedness to us, a generous attitude to debt, a confidence in God's forgiving love. That is the way to move forward in the spiritual life.

Prayer
We call you Father; we praise and bless you and gaze on your glory, which you would have us share; we pray for your kingdom to come and for the work of Jesus to be done among us; we know that you want to feed and care for us; and now we turn to

you and to our neighbour with new confidence and trust and pray for those we know and love, that they may share your vision and – with us – contemplate your love. Amen.

I am so certain of the guidance of God's hand that I hope to be maintained always in this certainty. You must never doubt that I walk thankfully and joyfully this path in which I am being led. My life in the past has been filled to overflowing with God's goodness, and above guilt stands the overflowing love of him who was crucified. I am most thankful of all for the people whom I have known, and hope only that they will never have to sorrow over me, and that they too will gratefully always be certain only of the kindness and forgiveness of God.

Dietrich Bonhoeffer, 1906–45

Be thou my vision, O Lord of my heart,
Be all else but naught to me, save that thou art;
Be thou my best thought in the day and the night,
Both waking and sleeping, thy presence my light.

High King of heaven, thou heaven's bright Sun,
O grant me its joys after vict'ry is won;
Great heart of my own heart, whatever befall,
Still be my vision, O Ruler of all.

Irish, 8th century, tr. Mary Byrne, 1880–1931

Exercise

If you are able to look at the night sky, think about it as a dense series of interconnected stars and watch them move and constellate. Imagine yourself within an equally intense but equally delicately balanced set of relationships and thank God for these.

If you cannot see the stars where you live, write down a list of the ten people you most love and sit down with it and thank God for them.

Tuesday – Week Five:
Naming our Sins –
as a Community

God is merciful and forgives us totally and utterly and unconditionally. That is why we can face up to our shared sinfulness.

Scripture Reading

The word of the Lord that came to Jeremiah concerning the drought: Judah mourns and her gates languish; they lie in gloom on the ground, and the cry of Jerusalem goes up. Her nobles send their servants for water; they come to the cisterns, they find no water, they return with their vessels empty. They are ashamed and dismayed and cover their heads, because the ground is cracked. Even the doe in the field forsakes her newborn fawn because there is no grass. The wild asses stand on the bare heights, they pant for air like jackals; their eyes fail because there is no herbage. Although our iniquities testify against us, act, O Lord, for your name's sake; our apostasies indeed are many, and we have sinned against you. O hope of Israel, its saviour in time of trouble, why should you be like a stranger in the land, like a traveller turning aside for the night? Why should you be like someone confused, like a mighty warrior who cannot give help? Yet you, O Lord, are in the midst of us, and we are called by your name; do not forsake us! (Jeremiah 14:1–9)

Reflection

When we pray for forgiveness with the words of the Lord's Prayer, we face up to collective as well as personal responsibility. The approaching millennium has a frightening dimension for some people for this very reason. They fear that our corporate sins will come home to roost. After all, they are easy enough to enumerate, and they affect the very categories of people and animals which Jeremiah listed in his account of the fall of Jerusalem. The Babylonians took Jerusalem in 587–586 BC, despite the political and religious warnings of Jeremiah who had raged away with prophetic words against the sins of the people and their leaders.

His account is like a snapshot photo and we look at it with the horror of recognition. Drought, distressed farmers, nature going berserk as the animals begin to suffer, the chain of birth and death in turmoil and then the sudden fear that God too has become a stranger, a traveller passing through who does not care. In Jeremiah's words, 'our iniquities testify against us'. The evidence of neglected relationships in our war-torn world, and of an exploitative attitude to the environment is all around us. We have sinned on a cosmic scale.

So what are we to do? Jeremiah again: 'Yet you, O Lord, are in the midst of us, and we are called by your name; do not forsake us!' We confess that we have done wrong and then we turn to God and ask to remember that he is with us in the mess we seem to have made. We ask to remember that we are called by the divine name; that we are the beloved of God; and that harmony can be restored. Simply to deny our problems, or to panic because they are so overwhelming is not enough. What we must do is turn to God with renewed conviction and say, 'Forgive us our sins for we ourselves forgive everyone indebted to us.'

Prayer
Almighty and ever-living God,
whose Son Jesus Christ healed the sick
and restored them to wholeness of life:
look with compassion on the anguish of the world,
and by your healing power
make whole both people and nations;
through our Lord Jesus Christ,
who is alive and reigns with you and the Holy Spirit,
one God, now and for ever, Amen.

Collect for 8th Sunday before Easter, ASB

High in the heavens, eternal God,
Thy goodness in full glory shines;
Thy truth shall break through every cloud
That veils and darkens thy designs.

For ever firm thy justice stands,
As mountains their foundations keep;
Wise are the wonders of thy hands;
Thy judgements are a mighty deep.

Thy providence is kind and large,
Both man and beast thy bounty share;
The whole creation is thy charge,
But saints are thy peculiar care.

My God, how excellent thy grace,
Whence all our hope and comfort springs!
The race of Adam in distress
Flies to the shadow of thy wings.

Life, like a fountain rich and free,
Springs from the presence of the Lord;
And in thy light our souls shall see
The glories promised by thy word.

Isaac Watts, 1674–1748

Exercise
Turn on the cold tap and run your hands under it as you say the
final verse of Isaac Watts' hymn to God the creator and
Redeemer. Notice what you feel.

Wednesday – Week Five: Reconciliation between the Nations

'For we ourselves forgive.' God's desire is to heal the world's pain.

Scripture Reading

Thus says the Lord: In a time of favour I have answered you, on a day of salvation I have helped you; I have kept you and given you as a covenant to the people, to establish the land, to apportion the desolate heritages; saying to the prisoners, 'Come out,' to those who are in darkness, 'Show yourselves.' They shall feed along the ways, on all the bare heights shall be their pasture; they shall not hunger or thirst, neither scorching wind nor sun shall strike them down, for he who has pity on them will lead them, and by springs of water will guide them. And I will turn all my mountains into a road, and my highways shall be raised up. Lo, these shall come from far away, and lo, these from the north and from the west, and these from the land of Syene. Sing for joy, O heavens, and exult, O earth; break forth, O mountains, into singing! For the Lord has comforted his people, and will have compassion on his suffering ones. (Isaiah 49:8–13)

Reflection

'On a day of salvation I have helped you.' Thus we examine what stands between us and the proper celebration of the resurrection. Sin, as we have seen, means denying our very humanity and separating ourselves from what makes us like other people. It means living a cocooned, isolated life. Grace and forgiveness bring us back into the shared story of God's relationships to the world and all its people.

Isaiah tells us that God answers our prayer for reconciliation. 'In a time of favour I have answered you, on a day of salvation I have helped you; I have kept you and given you as a covenant to the people.' These are powerful words, as they remind us that our salvation is wrapped up in that of other people. Our salvation becomes a covenant with everyone else. God heals us and expects us to work for the healing of the nations. The fact that we are healed or 'better' is bound up with the idea that other people can also aspire to be better.

What does this mean in practical terms? God hands out tasks to us. We are 'to establish the land, to apportion the desolate heritages; saying to the prisoners, "Come out," to those who are in darkness, "Show yourselves." ' This is not random piety, a catch-all of good intentions. A healed and reconciled people will do creative things with land, with debt, with prisoners, refugees and all those who are in darkness.

That is why the question of international debt and amnesties are part of our spiritual programme at the moment. When we receive so much ourselves from God, who are we to withhold generosity from the poor nations of the world? 'By their fruits you shall know them' (Matthew 7:16). That is what Isaiah was saying when he wrote, 'The Lord has comforted his people, and will have compassion on his suffering ones.' Our own comforting is bound up in God's compassion for his suffering ones. While one nation suffers, all remain bereft of true comfort.

Prayer

> Thou shalt know him
> When he comes
> Not by any din of drums
> Nor the vantage of his airs
> Nor by anything he wears
> Neither by his crown
> Nor his gown
> For his presence known shall be
> By the holy harmony
> That his coming makes in me.

Source unknown, 15th century

If we recall that Jesus came to 'preach the good news to the poor' (Matthew 11:5, Luke 7:22), how can we fail to lay greater emphasis on the Church's preferential option for the poor and the outcast? Indeed, it has to be said that a commitment to justice and peace in a world like ours, marked by so many conflicts and intolerable social and economic inequalities, is a necessary condition for the preparation and celebration of the Jubilee. Thus, in the spirit of the Book of Leviticus (25:8–12), Christians will have to raise their voice on behalf of the poor of the world, proposing the Jubilee as an appropriate time to give thought, among other things, to reducing substantially, if not cancelling outright, the international debt which seriously threatens the future of many nations.

Tertio Millennio Adveniente, John Paul II,
10 November 1994

Almighty Father,
whose will is to restore all things
in your beloved Son, the King of all:
govern the hearts and minds of those in authority,
and bring the families of the nations,
divided and torn apart by the ravages of sin,
to be subject to his just and gentle rule;
who is alive and reigns with you and the Holy Spirit,
one God, now and for ever.

Collect for Pentecost 15, ASB

Exercise
Look at a map of the world. Which country or countries do you
feel drawn to pray for? Why?

Thursday – Week Five: Reconciliation within Communities

'For we ourselves forgive everyone indebted to us.' God's desire is to heal pain and suffering where we experience it most closely.

Scripture Reading

I give thanks to my God always for you because of the grace of God that has been given you in Christ Jesus, for in every way you have been enriched in him, in speech and knowledge of every kind – just as the testimony of Christ has been strengthened among you – so that you are not lacking in any spiritual gift as you wait for the revealing of our Lord Jesus Christ. He will also strengthen you to the end, so that you may be blameless on the day of our Lord Jesus Christ. God is faithful; by him you were called into the fellowship of his Son, Jesus Christ our Lord. Now I appeal to you, brothers and sisters, by the name of our Lord Jesus Christ, that all of you be in agreement and that there be no divisions among you, but that you be united in the same mind and the same purpose. (1 Corinthians 1:4–10)

Reflection

The community to which Paul wrote this letter was a divided community. They also felt ambivalent towards Paul himself. He had lived with them for eighteen months, establishing his own personal authority with them as well as that of the gospel. Then he left them and went on to Ephesus. Internal wrangling broke out and soon affected every aspect of the Christian community's life. There were those who thought themselves perfect, those who thought that they were beyond the requirements of any law, those who were sexually immoral, those who refused to be conciliatory, those who were spiritual snobs and would not think about the needs of weaker Christians, the unconventional, the insensitive, the over-showy. The whole rag-bag of people who come together around a good project, but who bring themselves and their own problems with them.

His tone is tender. 'I give thanks to my God always for you because of the grace of God that has been given you in Christ Jesus, for in every way you have been enriched in him.' To blame people or wag a finger at them provokes guilt. And guilt does not bring us to freedom. Guilt is self-referring, it makes us brood on our sins instead of turning from them to the light. Paul knows that the only base from which to work for reconciliation is the shared sense of redemption. 'You are the beloved of God,' he reminds the people of Corinth and his words resonate through the centuries down to us. It is because of our status in the eyes of God that we can hear the deeper call, the call to 'be united in the same mind and the same purpose'.

True reconciliation demands that we seek out the mind and purpose which inspire us; that we remember the founding vision and live by it. Only then will we come to, and live in, the light.

Prayer

A Hymn to God the Father

Wilt Thou forgive that sin where I begun,
Which was my sin, though it were done before?
Wilt Thou forgive that sin, through which I run,
And do run still, though still I do deplore?
When Thou hast done, Thou hast not done,
    For I have more.

Wilt Thou forgive that sin by which I have won
Others to sin, and made my sin their door?
Wilt Thou forgive that sin which I did shun
A year, or two: but wallowed in, a score.
When Thou hast done, Thou hast not done,
    For I have more.

I have a sin of fear, that when I have spun
My last thread, I shall perish on the shore;
But swear by Thy self, that at my death Thy Son
Shall shine as he shines now, and heretofore;
And, having done that, Thou hast done;
    I fear no more.

John Donne, 1573–1631

Almighty God,
you have knit together your elect
into one communion and fellowship
in the mystical body of your Son.
Give us grace so to follow your blessed saints
in all virtuous and godly living,
that we may come to those unspeakable joys
which you have prepared for those who truly love you;
through Jesus Christ our Lord. Amen.

Collect for All Saints Day, ASB

Exercise

Write a list of the communities you belong to (your family or neighbourhood, friends, parish, workplace, car run and so on) and pray for reconciliation in each of them by name.

Friday – Week Five:
Jesus is our Redemption

'Forgive us our sins for we ourselves forgive everyone indebted to us.' We seek and find forgiveness in the saving work of Jesus.

Scripture Reading

Blessed be the God and Father of our Lord Jesus Christ, who has blessed us in Christ with every spiritual blessing in the heavenly places, just as he chose us in Christ before the foundation of the world to be holy and blameless before him in love. He destined us for adoption as his children through Jesus Christ, according to the good pleasure of his will, to the praise of his glorious grace that he freely bestowed on us in the Beloved. In him we have redemption through his blood, the forgiveness of our trespasses, according to the riches of his grace that he lavished on us. With all wisdom and insight he has made known to us the mystery of his will, according to his good pleasure that he set forth in Christ, as a plan for the fullness of time, to gather up all things in him, things in heaven and things on earth. (Ephesians 1:3–10)

Reflection

'In him we have redemption through his blood, the forgiveness of our trespasses.' Every time we pray the Lord's Prayer, we make a profession of faith. We say what we really believe.

Today's reading from Ephesians spells out the great overarching design of God; it reveals the very heart of God's desires for us: namely that we experience the fullness of salvation. Jesus died to take away our sins. And that work has been done. So now we are gathered up with all things in heaven and on earth, for the glory of God. The cycle of human disobedience has been broken through the obedience of the Son.

The language of redemption is not particularly popular nowadays. We are more comfortable with other aspects of the saving work of Jesus: we come more easily to the manger than to the cross; we are more enthusiastic about the work of creation than that of salvation. Traditional Christian spirituality asks for balance. It says that each of the saving mysteries needs to be kept in tension with the others, so that they talk to each other and hold us at the place of desire. Contemporary Christian spirituality also wants to bring us to this place of desire. It too has an important message. It says that we do not come here alone; we accompany each other to the foot of the cross. Ours is a personal journey, but not a private one, for my redemption and your redemption are bound up with each other. With this insight in mind, it is possible to return to some of the old hymns and texts and read them with new eyes. They know about desire and passion – and the Passion and the desire of God.

Prayer

> Blessed assurance, Jesus is mine:
> O what a foretaste of glory divine!
> Heir of salvation, purchase of God;
> Born of his Spirit, washed in his blood:
> *This is my story, this is my song,*
> *Praising my Saviour all the day long.*
>
> Perfect submission, perfect delight,
> Visions of rapture burst on my sight;
> Angels descending bring from above
> Echoes of mercy, whispers of love:

Perfect submission, all is at rest,
I in my Saviour am happy and blest –
Watching and waiting, looking above,
Filled with his goodness, lost in his
love:

Frances Jane van Alstyne, 1820–1915

Almighty, ever-living God,
you have given the human race Jesus Christ our Saviour
as a model of humility.
He fulfilled your will
by becoming man and giving his life on the cross.
Help us to bear witness to you
by following his example of suffering
and make us worthy to share in his resurrection.
We ask this through Jesus Christ, your Son,
who lives and reigns with you and the Holy Spirit,
one God, for ever and ever. Amen.

Collect for Passion Sunday, Roman Missal

Exercise

As we prepare for the final week and begin to think about the
events of the passion and death of Jesus, ask yourself who you
would like to be: one of the disciples – deeply engaged in the
story, but judged by it because you know that you will be shown
up as a betrayer or a coward; one of the women who followed
Jesus, and then proved powerless to protect him; a detached
bystander, the witness who has no particular investment in what
happens next; an ordinary citizen of Jerusalem who simply gets
on with life and neither knows nor cares what happens to Jesus;
someone else? In the Holy Week tableau, where do you stand?

Saturday – Week Five: Waiting upon God's Forgiveness

'Forgive us our sins for we ourselves forgive everyone indebted to us.' We receive God's forgiveness.

Scripture Reading

The Lord is merciful and gracious, slow to anger and abounding in steadfast love. He will not always accuse, nor will he keep his anger forever. He does not deal with us according to our sins, nor repay us according to our iniquities. For as the heavens are high above the earth, so great is his steadfast love toward those who fear him; as far as the east is from the west, so far he removes our transgressions from us. As a father has compassion for his children, so the Lord has compassion for those who fear him. (Psalm 103:8–13)

Reflection

'The Lord is merciful and gracious.' Today we rest in the knowledge that God is merciful towards us. The psalmist uses two comparisons to describe the immensity of God's forgiving love. Both are spatial. Both draw on nature. One is about the distance between heaven and earth; the other is about the distance between one skyline and another. These are immovable, unnegotiable, given. No amount of tinkering around can move earth closer to heaven or heaven closer to earth. Mirages may play around with our sense of horizon, but the true boundaries of our universe remain constant. So the vault of heaven and the furthest of our horizons become a huge measuring tape: the one tells us that God loves us and the other that God forgives us. That data is rock solid. Nothing can change it.

Once this knowledge begins to sink in we can turn back to the Lord's Prayer with a new sense of release. We can begin to receive its message. And with new energy we too can begin to look at forgiveness and our need to give it as well as to receive it. If this is how wonderful being merciful is, how can we refuse it to other people? Forgiveness is a costly business, it strips away our sense of self-righteousness. We recognise our own errors, our own collusion, our own pigheadedness. It keeps us sane and brings freedom to those whom we forgive.

'Forgive and forget,' people say. But that is mistaken. The Judaeo-Christian tradition treasures memory and knows the power of storytelling. We have to forgive and remember, for otherwise we are likely to repeat ourselves. As we move towards Holy Week, the week when we consciously remember what happened to Jesus in Jerusalem as he faced betrayal and death, we do not gloss over the facts. Each detail is immeasurably important. It discloses meaning to us; it confirms the depth of his commitment to the human condition. Without memory, we would have no knowledge of salvation. That is why the tradition treasures memory so.

But it also knows that we can learn from our own past, and that our sins and failings and mistakes are important to us now. Like the high heavens and the vanishing skyline, they are the mirror into which we gaze when we need to remember God's love and forgiveness of us.

Prayer

Beneath the cross of Jesus
I fain would take my stand –
The shadow of a mighty rock
Within a weary land;
A home within a wilderness,
A rest upon the way,
From the burning of the noontide heat
And the burden of the day.

O safe and happy shelter,
O refuge tried and sweet,
O trysting-place where heaven's love
And heaven's justice meet!
As to the holy patriarch
That wondrous dream was given,
So seems my Saviour's cross to me
A ladder up to heaven.

I take, O cross, thy shadow,
For my abiding-place!
I ask no other sunshine than
The sunshine of his face;
Content to let the world go by,
To know no gain or loss –
My sinful self my only shame,
My glory all – the cross.

                              Elizabeth Cecilia Clephane, 1830–69

Everlasting God,
who in your tender love towards the human race
sent your Son our Saviour Jesus Christ to take upon him our
    flesh
and to suffer death upon the cross:
grant that we may follow the example of his patience and
    humility,
and also be made partakers of his resurrection;
through Jesus Christ our Lord.

Collect for Palm Sunday, ASB

Exercise

Go and look at the sky and look at the horizon. Remember the words, 'As the heavens are high above the earth, so great is his steadfast love toward those who fear him; as far as the east is from the west, so far he removes our transgressions from us.'

6th Sunday –
The Time of Trial and
God's Response

With the beginning of Holy Week comes a new opportunity to consider the saving work of Jesus, the son who is sent to the Lord's vineyard.

Scripture Reading

'Listen to another parable. There was a landowner who planted a vineyard, put a fence around it, dug a wine press in it, and built a watchtower. Then he leased it to tenants and went to another country. When the harvest time had come, he sent his slaves to the tenants to collect his produce. But the tenants seized his slaves and beat one, killed another, and stoned another. Again he sent other slaves, more than the first; and they treated them in the same way. Finally he sent his son to them, saying, "They will respect my son." But when the tenants saw the son, they said to themselves, "This is the heir; come, let us kill him and get his inheritance." So they seized him, threw him out of the vineyard, and killed him. Now when the owner of the vineyard comes, what will he do to those tenants?' They said to him, 'He will put those wretches to a miserable death, and lease the vineyard to other tenants who will give him the produce at the harvest time.' Jesus said to them, 'Have you never read in the Scriptures: "The stone that the builders rejected

has become the cornerstone; this was the Lord's doing,
and it is amazing in our eyes"?' (Matthew 21:33–42)

Reflection

This parable appears in Matthew, Mark and Luke. It is a key to
understanding many of the great gospel themes which come to
their climax in the final week of Jesus's life. The vineyard of the
Lord's planting is a theme beloved of the Hebrew Scriptures. It is
a place of promise, richness and deliverance. Yet in this story it
becomes a place of betrayal. For the tenants who had charge of
the vineyard failed in their task of stewardship. They were jealous
of the rights of their master over them, questioning his authority
and subverting its demands. They killed and stoned and beat up
the messengers whom he sent to them. And then they destroyed
his son, casting him out of the vineyard to his death.

Traditionally this has been read as a story of the rejection of
Jesus by God's chosen people, the Jews. Just as they had rejected
the prophets who had been sent to them in Old Testament times,
now they reject the Son. Matthew, in particular, would have an
interest in exploring this meaning in the text. But nowadays we
are embarrassed by it. We know far more about the horrendous
consequences of anti-Semitism to feel comfortable about using
the Scriptures to sanction it. We are all too aware of our own
tendency to reject the messengers whom God sends to us. We
know about our own infidelity to the Word of God made known
to us in Jesus. We know about our own capacity to reject God's
authority. The events of Holy Week did not simply happen then,
back in Jerusalem. They happen nowadays as well. It is we who
join the crowds who acclaim Jesus today and then betray him
so effortlessly tomorrow and the next day. We are implicated in
this story too.

Holy Week gives us an opportunity to reflect on the great
themes of our salvation. This can look like a daunting task, because
it is so easy to be driven by guilt rather than love. So how are we
to go with Jesus to his suffering and death? How can we safely
stay with him during his time of trial? The only way is the way of
love. Let us pray with the words of the prophet Isaiah.

Prayer

'Let me sing for my beloved my love-song concerning his
vineyard: My beloved had a vineyard on a very fertile hill. He
dug it and cleared it of stones, and planted it with choice
vines; he built a watchtower in the midst of it, and hewed out
a wine vat in it; he expected it to yield grapes, but it yielded
wild grapes. And now, inhabitants of Jerusalem and people of
Judah, judge between me and my vineyard. What more was there
to do for my vineyard that I have not done in it? When I expected
it to yield grapes, why did it yield wild grapes? And now I
will tell you what I will do to my vineyard. I will remove its
hedge, and it shall be devoured; I will break down its wall,
and it shall be trampled down. I will make it a waste; it shall
not be pruned or hoed, and it shall be overgrown with briers
and thorns; I will also command the clouds that they rain
no rain upon it. For the vineyard of the Lord of hosts is
the house of Israel, and the people of Judah are his pleasant
planting.'

(Isaiah 5:1–7)

God our Father,
in the transfigured glory of Christ your Son,
you strengthened our faith
by confirming the witness of your prophets,
and show us the splendour of your beloved sons and daughters.
As we listen to the voice of your Son,
help us to become heirs to eternal life with him
who lives and reigns with you and the Holy spirit,
one God, for ever and ever, Amen.

Feast of the Transfiguration, Roman Missal

Exercise

Consider the ways in which God has been persistently faithful
to you. Recall some of the messengers he has sent into your
life. For example, people who have helped us grow or who have
comforted us. Pray in thanksgiving for the gift of his Son and
ask for the grace to let him into your vineyard.

Monday – Week Six:
Our own Trials

We reflect on our own trials as Jesus faces the time of trial.

Scripture Reading

My brothers and sisters, whenever you face trials of any kind, consider it nothing but joy, because you know that the testing of your faith produces endurance; and let endurance have its full effect, so that you may be mature and complete, lacking in nothing. If any of you is lacking in wisdom, ask God, who gives to all. But ask in faith, never doubting, for the one who doubts is like a wave of the sea, driven and tossed by the wind; for the doubter, being double-minded and unstable in every way, must not expect to receive anything from the Lord. Let the believer who is lowly boast in being raised up, and the rich in being brought low, because the rich will disappear like a flower in the field. For the sun rises with its scorching heat and withers the field; its flower falls, and its beauty perishes. It is the same way with the rich; in the midst of a busy life, they will wither away. Blessed is anyone who endures temptation. Such a one has stood the test and will receive the crown of life that the Lord has promised to those who love him. (James 1:2–12)

Reflection

'Blessed is anyone who endures temptation.' 'Let endurance have its full effect, so that you may be mature and complete, lacking in nothing.' The time of trial is a time of testing and growth. James writes his letter for a growing, though persecuted, Church. He is concerned with the trials faced corporately by a group whose identity is under threat from outsiders who oppose it and from insiders who threaten its unity. We read this text as individuals, but can still be helped by its double focus. Trials come from without and from within.

Human sadness and pain, anxiety and illness are all around us. Sometimes they afflict us personally. As we begin to reflect on the final week of Jesus's earthly life, we do well to take stock, to identify our own pain and stress points, so that we can bring them to prayer. But James exhorts us to do more than that. He invites us to look inside as well and see how we persecute ourselves. He calls this 'doubt' and warns us off it, because it will destroy us.

We all face temptation. It is part of the human condition and we grow on account of it, not despite it. What catches us off our guard and destroys us is giving in to doubt and despair. James's word is old-fashioned: he calls for endurance – and, at our most desperate, so do we. This week we pray for endurance, for that rock-solid quality that sustains us even in despair. Then, when we pray the Lord's Prayer, we do so knowingly, with the full weight that goes with understanding the cost of any time of trial. We do not pray lightly, and so we will not pray in vain.

Prayer
All-powerful God,
by the suffering and death of your Son,
strengthen and protect us in our weakness.
We ask this through Our Lord Jesus Christ, your Son,
who lives and reigns with you and the Holy Spirit,
one God, for ever and ever, Amen.

                    Collect for Monday of Holy Week, Roman Missal

When I survey the wondrous cross,
On which the Prince of glory died,
My richest gain I count but loss,
And pour contempt on all my pride.

Forbid it, Lord, that I should boast
Save in the death of Christ my God;
All the vain things that charm me most,
I sacrifice them to his blood.

See from his head, his hands, his feet,
Sorrow and love flow mingled down;
Did e'er such love and sorrow meet,
Or thorns compose so rich a crown?

His dying crimson, like a robe,
Spreads o'er his body on the tree;
Then am I dead to all the globe,
And all the globe is dead to me.

Were the whole realm of nature mine,
That were a present far too small;
Love so amazing, so divine,
Demands my soul, my life, my all.

                                        Isaac Watts, 1674–1748

Exercise
Allow yourself to remember a time of trial in your own life and
thank God for your own endurance. Say again, slowly, 'And do
not bring us to the time of trial,' thanking God for the endurance
of Jesus.

Tuesday – Week Six:
The Trials of Jesus

We go with Jesus to his time of trial.

Scripture Reading

They went to a place called Gethsemane; and Jesus said
to his disciples, 'Sit here while I pray.' He took with
him Peter and James and John, and began to be
distressed and agitated. And said to them, 'I am deeply
grieved, even to death; remain here, and keep awake.'
And going a little farther, he threw himself on the
ground and prayed that, if it were possible, the hour
might pass from him. He said, 'Abba, Father, for you
all things are possible; remove this cup from me; yet,
not what I want, but what you want.' He came and found
them sleeping; and he said to Peter, 'Simon, are you
asleep? Could you not keep awake one hour? Keep
awake and pray that you may not come into the time of
trial; the spirit indeed is willing, but the flesh is weak.'
And again he went away and prayed, saying the same
words. And once more he came and found them
sleeping, for their eyes were very heavy; and they did
not know what to say to him. He came a third time and
said to them, 'Are you still sleeping and taking your
rest? Enough! The hour has come; the Son of Man is
betrayed into the hands of sinners. Get up, let us be
going. See, my betrayer is at hand.' (Mark 14:32–42)

Reflection

The distress and grief of Jesus comfort us. Whatever happens to us, and wherever it happens, he has been there before us. He has felt abandoned by his closest friends and tested by God. He has tasted the bitter gall of Gethsemane and known the full force of failure. Mark makes a careful use of verbs in his text. Up until this point in the gospel, Jesus has been the subject of the verbs he uses. Jesus has spoken and walked and given and blessed. He has seen and heard, prayed and observed. Now the opposite is about to happen. From this story onwards Jesus will be the object of verbs and not their subject. He will be taken, stripped, crucified. And here at Gethsemane the disempowerment begins.

Is this the cup he prays to be spared? After all, it is the hardest one of all. Up until this point he has been sustained by a vision, he has known that he was doing the Father's will. All the energy and enthusiasm he put into the three years of preaching and teaching and healing in Galilee, in Judea and beyond were directed towards proclaiming a bright kingdom which would bring people to freedom. That was the message he proclaimed. And now? Now he faces the collapse of all his dreams. This is a truly bitter cup. The end of one way of calling people to belief in the goodness of God; the beginning of another. No wonder he calls it the time of trial. For both the spirit and the flesh take sides and he is torn between the two.

Prayer

O Jesus, poor and abject, unknown and despised, have mercy upon me, and let me not be ashamed to follow thee.

O Jesus, hated, calumniated, and persecuted, have mercy upon me, and make me content to be as my master.

O Jesus, blasphemed, accused, and wrongfully condemned, have mercy upon me, and teach me to endure the contradiction of sinners.

O Jesus, clothed with a habit of reproach and shame, have mercy upon me, and let me not seek my own glory.

O Jesus, insulted, mocked, and spat upon, have mercy upon

me, and let me not faint in the fiery trial.

O Jesus, crowned with thorns and hailed in derision;

O Jesus burdened with our sins and the curses of the people;

O Jesus, affronted, outraged, buffeted, overwhelmed with injuries, griefs and humiliations;

O Jesus, hanging on the accursed tree, bowing the head, giving up the ghost, have mercy upon me, and conform my whole soul to thy holy, humble, suffering Spirit.

John Wesley, 1703–91

Father,
may we receive your forgiveness and mercy
as we celebrate the passion and death of the Lord,
who lives and reigns with you and the Holy Spirit,
one God, for ever and ever, Amen.

Collect for Tuesday of Holy Week, Roman Missal

> Alone with none but thee, my God,
> I journey on my way.
> What need I fear, when thou art near
> O king of night and day?
> More safe am I within thy hand
> Than if a host did round me stand.

Columba, 521–97

Exercise

Say slowly, 'Not my will, but thine be done.' And then repeat St Columba's prayer.

Wednesday – Week Six: Betrayal

We go with Jesus to his betrayal.

Scripture Reading

While Jesus was still speaking, Judas, one of the twelve, arrived; with him was a large crowd with swords and clubs, from the chief priests and the elders of the people. Now the betrayer had given them a sign, saying, 'The one I will kiss is the man; arrest him.' At once he came up to Jesus and said, 'Greetings, Rabbi!' and kissed him. Jesus said to him, 'Friend, do what you are here to do.' Then they came and laid hands on Jesus and arrested him. Suddenly, one of those with Jesus put his hand on his sword, drew it, and struck the slave of the high priest, cutting off his ear. Then Jesus said to him, 'Put your sword back into its place; for all who take the sword will perish by the sword. Do you think that I cannot appeal to my Father, and he will at once send me more than twelve legions of angels? But how then would the Scriptures be fulfilled, which say it must happen in this way?' At that hour Jesus said to the crowds, 'Have you come out with swords and clubs to arrest me as though I were a bandit? Day after day I sat in the temple teaching, and you did not arrest me. But all this has taken place, so that the Scriptures of the prophets may be fulfilled.' Then all the disciples deserted him and fled. (Matthew 26:47–56)

Reflection

Matthew tells us about the betrayal of Jesus by Judas and his subsequent desertion as all the disciples flee. Now nothing stands between him and the cross.

When he first called them, they followed him so enthusiastically. When he first sent them out to preach in pairs, they returned on such a high. When he sat them down on the ground and taught and fed them, they were all over him. And now he is going to death, they run away. We read this story with a growing sense of unease. These people, these disciples, these followers of the Lord, are so incredibly like us. We know all about fidelity in time of joy and celebration. But when the people we love begin to fail, or to get old or ill, or to die, our faith is tested. We are less enamoured of failure than we are of success.

Jesus is betrayed by the people who are close to him, not by some disinterested outsider. That is why the betrayal hurts. Only a friend can give such a bitter blow. Only a lover can betray with a kiss.

When did the betrayal begin? When did Judas begin to question the work of Jesus? When did greed creep into his soul? We do not know. But this week we have reason to reflect on the prophetic nature of Jesus's own prayer, when he taught his followers to say, 'And do not bring us to the time of trial.' Words we need to say again and again.

Prayer

All who hate me whisper together about me; they imagine the worst for me.

They think that a deadly thing has fastened on me, that I will not rise again from where I lie.

Even my bosom friend in whom I trusted, who ate of my bread, has lifted the heel against me.

But you, O Lord, be gracious to me, and raise me up, that I may repay them.

By this I know that you are pleased with me; because my enemy has not triumphed over me.

But you have upheld me because of my integrity, and set me in
   your presence forever.
Blessed be the Lord, the God of Israel, from everlasting to
   everlasting. Amen and Amen.

Psalm 41:7–13

In the Lord's atoning grief
Be our rest and sweet relief;
Deep within our hearts we'll store
Those dear pains and wrongs he bore.

Thorns and cross and nails and spear,
Wounds that faithful hearts revere,
Vinegar and gall and reed
And the pang his soul that freed.

May these all our spirits fill,
And with love inflame our will;
Plant in us contrition's root,
Ripen there its saving fruit.

Crucified, we thee adore,
Thee with all our hearts implore;
With the saints our souls unite
In the realms of heavenly light.

Christ, by coward hands betrayed,
Christ, for us a captive made,
Christ, upon the bitter tree,
Slain for man, be praise to thee.

Bonaventure, 1221–74

Exercise
Pray today for people who are tempted to despair; those who
believe that they are beyond the reach of God's love.

Thursday – Week Six:
The Last Supper

Jesus begins his passion.

Scripture Reading

When the hour came, he took his place at the table, and the apostles with him. He said to them, 'I have eagerly desired to eat this Passover with you before I suffer; for I tell you, I will not eat it until it is fulfilled in the kingdom of God.' Then he took a cup, and after giving thanks he said, 'Take this and divide it among yourselves; for I tell you that from now on I will not drink of the fruit of the vine until the kingdom of God comes.' Then he took a loaf of bread, and when he had given thanks, he broke it and gave it to them, saying, 'This is my body, which is given for you. Do this in remembrance of me.' And he did the same with the cup after supper, saying, 'This cup that is poured out for you is the new covenant in my blood.' (Luke 22:14–22)

Reflection

Today we keep a feast day. Maundy Thursday is the beginning of the Easter Triduum, the three days which mark Christ's passage through death to glory. If we are to understand Easter, we need to understand each bit of Jesus's story as he experiences it. For like a series of icons, the different parts of this drama speak to each other and explain each other to us. One story is a mirror into which we look to understand the other and the whole.

So today Jesus does to the bread what will be done to him tomorrow. He takes, blesses, breaks and gives it to his friends. He does the same with the cup, giving it with a blessing, just as his own blood will be given tomorrow. No wonder the two stories are mirror images of each other. No wonder today's is the story we re-enact at every Eucharist. For what we celebrate today is total love and total self-gift.

Jesus gives himself to us to be our life and our salvation. He risks the naked encounter of true love. Such love desires the goodness of the beloved; it seeks us out and recognises and knows us. It becomes our food and drink, and hammers at the gates of our souls. That is why the Christian tradition has turned to the language of passion and desire to try to explain Jesus's death to us. It uses the telling image, such as the pelican who feeds its young from its own breast. It turns to poetry for inspiration. In the Song of Songs, for example, we read of the tenderness of such love: 'I am my beloved's and my beloved is mine; he pastures his flock among the lilies' (Song 6:3); and of the fierce passion of true desire: 'Set me as a seal upon your heart, as a seal upon your arm; for love is strong as death, passion fierce as the grave. Its flashes are flashes of fire, a raging flame. Many waters cannot quench love, neither can floods drown it' (Song 8:4–6).

'Love is strong as death.' That is what Jesus will prove tomorrow. For today, let us rest in the certainty that he sets us as a seal upon his heart, and that we may do the same with him.

Prayer

All-holy Father, king of endless glory,
faithful Creator, look on your creation:
Singing we praise you in this banquet given
for our salvation.

Now we remember how your servant Jesus
fed his companions, bread and wine supplying;
gave them his presence in these holy tokens,
pledge of his dying.

Father, we bless you in this celebration:
praise for the body broken for our healing,
praise for the sacred blood of our redemption,
mercy revealing.

Hear our petitions which we bring before you:
guard us in weakness – comfort the forsaken,
strengthen the tempted; give to all the faithful
victory unshaken.

                                    Angela Tilby, 1950–

O God, who in this wondrous sacrament hast left unto us a
memorial of thy passion; grant us so to venerate the sacred
mysteries of thy body and blood, that we may ever continue to
feel within ourselves the blessed fruit of thy redemption. Who
livest and reignest God, for ever and ever, Amen.

O loving Pelican! O Jesu Lord!
Unclean I am, but cleanse me in thy blood;
Of which a single drop, for sinners spilt,
Is ransom for a world's entire guilt.

                                    Thomas Aquinas, 1225–74

Exercise
Listen to Jesus as he says these words to you: 'I have eagerly
desired to eat this Passover with you before I suffer; for I tell
you, I will not eat it until it is fulfilled in the kingdom of God.'

Friday – Week Six:
Jesus the Bread who is Given

Jesus dies on the cross.

Scripture Reading

After this, when Jesus knew that all was now finished,
he said (in order to fulfil the Scripture), 'I am thirsty.'
A jar full of sour wine was standing there. So they put
a sponge full of the wine on a branch of hyssop and
held it to his mouth. When Jesus had received the wine,
he said, 'It is finished.' Then he bowed his head and
gave up his spirit. (John 19:28–30)

Reflection

'It is finished,' says Jesus. He bows his head and gives up his
spirit. Each year brings us inexorably to this point. This is
where everything Jesus did in his life gains its meaning. This is
where everything we do in our lives is judged and finds its
meaning.

He was taken, blessed, broken and now he is given, handed
over to death for our salvation. We share his sufferings, we grieve
with his mother and the beloved disciple as they stand at the
foot of the cross, we repeat the words 'And do not bring us to
the time of trial,' but we do so in utter confidence. Because now
we know that God loves us. This is the evidence; this is the
proof.

That is why we need to stand at this place and absorb its
meaning.

'For he grew up before him like a young plant, and like a root out of dry ground; he had no form or majesty that we should look at him, nothing in his appearance that we should desire him. He was despised and rejected by others; a man of suffering and acquainted with infirmity; and as one from whom others hide their faces he was despised, and we held him of no account. Surely he has borne our infirmities and carried our diseases; yet we accounted him stricken, struck down by God, and afflicted. But he was wounded for our transgressions, crushed for our iniquities; upon him was the punishment that made us whole, and by his bruises we are healed' (Isaiah 53:25).

'He was wounded for our transgressions.' When Jesus says, 'It is finished' the burden of guilt and blame is lifted from us; we are made whole, we are healed. His life ends in death. Our own life begins. We receive grace upon grace; every grace, 'pressed down, shaken together, running over'; this is not simply a time, it is a moment to receive. The cross becomes a burning bush, a place of disclosure, revelation. Take your stand with Mary and the beloved disciple for here we are known as nowhere else. Here we are safe, here we are saved.

Prayer

> O Love divine, what hast thou done!
> The immortal God hath died for me!
> The Father's co-eternal Son
> Bore all my sins upon the tree;
> The immortal God for me hath died!
> My Lord, my Love is crucified –
>
> Is crucified for me and you,
> To bring us rebels back to God;
> Believe, believe the record true,
> We all are bought with Jesu's blood,
> Pardon for all flows from his side:
> My Lord, my Love is crucified.

Then let us stand beneath the cross,
And feel his love a healing stream,
All things for him account but loss,
And give up all your hearts to him;
Of nothing think or speak beside:
My Lord, my Love is crucified.

Charles Wesley, 1707–88

Lord,
by shedding his blood for us,
your Son, Jesus Christ,
established the paschal mystery.
In your goodness, make us holy
and watch over us always.
We ask this through Christ our Lord, Amen.

Collect for Good Friday, Roman Missal

My people, what have I done to you?
How have I offended you? Answer me!
    I led you out of Egypt, from slavery to freedom,
    but you led your Saviour to the cross.
Holy is God. Holy and strong. Holy immortal One,
have mercy on us!

Good Friday Reproaches, Roman Missal

Exercise
Make the time to absorb today's mystery. In your imagination
stand at the foot of the cross and watch Jesus die.

Saturday – Week Six:
Waiting at the Tomb

We watch and wait and feel our loss.

Scripture Reading

Now there was a good and righteous man named Joseph, who, though a member of the council, had not agreed to their plan and action. He came from the Jewish town of Arimathea, and he was waiting expectantly for the kingdom of God. This man went to Pilate and asked for the body of Jesus. Then he took it down, wrapped it in a linen cloth, and laid it in a rock-hewn tomb where no one had ever been laid. It was the day of Preparation, and the sabbath was beginning. The women who had come with him from Galilee followed, and they saw the tomb and how his body was laid. Then they returned, and prepared spices and ointments. On the sabbath they rested according to the commandment. (Luke 23:50–56)

Reflection

When Jesus died, his mother, Mary the wife of Clopas and Mary Magdalen, and his followers had watched it happen. Powerless to help, they had undergone his stripping and crucifixion and death. Then he was taken down from the cross and placed in a new tomb, the entrance sealed. Then the clock had moved inexorably on. Good Friday turns into Holy Saturday. Numbed and dismayed by turns, in common with all who grieve, his friends had watched the shadows lengthen. Their sense of abandonment was focused on a sealed tomb.

Each of the accounts of the passion of Jesus has details which vary from the others. But the story of the intervention of Joseph of Arimathea is common to all four gospels. Here was the good, loyal follower who used his influence to have Jesus decently buried. During his life, Joseph had followed him secretly; now Jesus is dead he does so openly. The process of transformation has begun.

As though to emphasise this, Luke uses the language of hope and of change in his account. Joseph was a man who 'was waiting expectantly for the kingdom of God'. Expectation is in the air. He took the body of Jesus and 'laid it in a rock-hewn tomb where no one had ever been laid'. A new tomb for a new experience. Luke tells us that it was the Day of Preparation, that the sabbath time of encounter with God was beginning. Today, Holy Saturday, becomes a day of rest and a day of anticipation.

The tradition gives it another theme as well. We may be resting but Jesus is not. The work of redemption is now in place and the first to experience it are those who waited for it the longest. Medieval mystery plays show scenes of Jesus 'harrowing hell'. He goes down among the dead, stirs them up and winnows a harvest among them. The prophets and patriarchs are recognised and called to glory. Their time of trial is over, and so too is ours.

Prayer

> Love's redeeming work is done;
> Fought the fight, the battle won:
> Lo, our Sun's eclipse is o'er!
> Lo, he sets in blood no more.
>
> Vain the stone, the watch, the seal,
> Christ has burst the gates of hell;
> Death in vain forbids his rise;
> Christ has opened Paradise.

Lives again our glorious King;
Where, O death, is now thy sting?
Dying once he all doth save;
Where thy victory, O grave?

Charles Wesley, 1707–88

May he support us all the day long till the shades lengthen and
the evening comes, and the busy world is hushed, and the fever
of life is over and our work is done, then, in his mercy, may he
give us a safe lodging, and a holy rest and peace at the last.

John Henry Newman, 1801–90

Today a tomb holds him who holds the creation in the hollow
of his hand; a stone covers him who covered the heavens with
glory. Life sleeps and hell trembles, and Adam is set free from
his bonds. Glory to thy dispensation, whereby thou hast accom-
plished all things, granting us an eternal Sabbath, thy most holy
Resurrection from the dead.

What is this sight we behold? What is this present rest? The
King of the ages, having through his passion fulfilled the plan
of salvation, keeps Sabbath in the tomb, granting us a new
Sabbath. Unto him let us cry aloud: Arise O Lord, judge thou
the earth, for measureless is thy great mercy and thou dost reign
for ever.

Come let us see our Life lying in the tomb, that he may give
life to those that in their tombs lie dead. Come, let us look today
on the Son of Judah as he sleeps, and with the prophet let us cry
aloud to him: Thou hast slept as a lion; who will awaken thee, O
King? But of thine own free will do thou rise up, who willingly
dost give thyself for us, O Lord, glory to thee. Amen

Mattins for Holy Saturday, Orthodox Liturgy

Exercise
Enjoy some rest today.

Final Sunday –
Resurrection

Christ is risen from the dead. Amen. Alleluia!

Scripture Reading

What then are we to say? Should we continue in sin in order that grace may abound? By no means! How can we who died to sin go on living in it? Do you not know that all of us who have been baptised into Christ Jesus were baptised into his death? Therefore we have been buried with him by baptism into death, so that, just as Christ was raised from the dead by the glory of the Father, so we too might walk in newness of life. For if we have been united with him in a death like his, we will certainly be united with him in a resurrection like his. We know that our old self was crucified with him so that the body of sin might be destroyed, and we might no longer be enslaved to sin. For whoever has died is freed from sin. But if we have died with Christ, we believe that we will also live with him. We know that Christ, being raised from the dead, will never die again; death no longer has dominion over him. The death he died, he died to sin, once for all; but the life he lives, he lives to God. So you also must consider yourselves dead to sin and alive to God in Christ Jesus. (Romans 6:1–11)

Reflection

This then is the meaning of Lent and of Easter. A time to receive the love of God, the life of Christ and the freedom of the Holy Spirit. With his disciples we make our way to the empty tomb. With them we recognise the Risen Christ in a variety of encounters. He meets us where we are: on a road, by a lake, behind our sealed doors, in our own homes. Jesus is risen from the dead. He is with us.

'But if we have died with Christ, we believe that we will also live with him.' Paul explores the meaning of the resurrection. He demonstrates that it is something that happens to us and which we live out within our own reality. It is for here and now. It happens today. It happens in us. We have died with Christ and each year we re-enact that reality. It brings us to the foot of the cross. We go down into the tomb with Christ. And today we rise with him and enjoy his risen life in its fullness. That is what 'living with him' means.

Without the passion there would be no resurrection. 'If we have been united with him in a death like his, we will certainly be united with him in a resurrection like his.' What is this death? Baptism, Paul explains. The descent into the waters of baptism. He describes it as a burial: 'Therefore we have been buried with him by baptism into death.' This is awesome and frightening, which is why Paul goes on to explain that something so powerful was necessary. 'Our old self was crucified with him so that the body of sin might be destroyed, and we might no longer be enslaved to sin.' By baptism into the death of Christ, we have been set free from our slavery to sin.

That is what the new life of the resurrection is all about: 'So you also must consider yourselves dead to sin and alive to God in Christ Jesus.' Jesus Christ meets our deepest desires. We are alive to God in him.

Prayer

Lord of all life and power,
who through the mighty resurrection of your Son
overcame the old order of sin and death to make all things new
    in him:
grant that we, being dead to sin and alive to you in Jesus Christ,
may reign with him in glory;
to whom with you and the Holy Spirit be praise and honour,
    glory and might,
now and in all eternity.

Collect for Easter Sunday, ASB

Christians, to the Paschal Victim offer sacrifice and praise.
The sheep are ransomed by the Lamb;
and Christ, the undefiled,
hath sinners to his Father reconciled.
Death with life contending: combat strangely ended!
Life's own Champion, slain, yet lives to reign.
Tell us, Mary: say what thou didst see upon the way.
The tomb the Living did enclose;
I saw Christ's glory as he rose!
The angels were attesting;
shroud with grave-clothes resting.
Christ, my hope, has risen: he goes before you into Galilee.
That Christ is truly risen from the dead we know.
Victorious King, thy mercy show!
Amen.

Victimae Paschali laudes, The Easter Sequence,
Roman Missal

    Stand by us, Lord,
    Give us peace,
    courage and bright hopes,
    This day and all our days.

Angela Tilby, 1950–

Exercise

Thank God for all the graces you have received over the past forty-three days. Thank God for your own faithful observance of this 'time to receive'. Thank God for all the people who have prayed with you and for you. And say once again the words from Luke 11:2–4:

> Father,
> hallowed be your name.
> Your kingdom come.
> Give us each day our daily bread.
> And forgive us our sins,
> for we ourselves forgive
> everyone indebted to us.
> And do not bring us to the time of trial.
> Amen.

Index

Hymns

Prayers